ARCHTYPE *of the* SPIRIT

Akhenaton offering sacrifice to Aton, Egyptian Museum, Cairo.

ARCHTYPE *of the* SPIRIT

Origins of Spirituality
—Individual & Collective

by

Peter Tufts Richardson

RED BARN PUBLISHING
Rockland, Maine

Published by
RED BARN PUBLISHING
22 Mechanic Street
Rockland, ME 04841-3514
www.redbarnrockland.com

ISBN-10: 0-9741152-2-3
ISBN-13: 978-0-9741152-2-1

Book and cover Design by Amy Fischer Design Associates, Camden, ME
Illustrations by Dobromil Nosek, Camden, ME
Printed by Custom Museum Publishing, Rockland, Maine

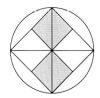

CONTENTS

Tree at shore, Acadia National Park,
Mt. Desert, Maine.

To

my mother and aunt

Eleanor (Pearson) Richardson

and

Dorothy Pearson

who by example inspired in me the habit of reading.

Figure holding Ankh, symbol of life, Luxor Temple, Egypt.

PREFACE

To experience a deep reality, which as it were comes at you out of the blue, from some remote place, requires a response. I felt the presence of what I am calling the Archetype of the Spirit through so many avenues I feel I can no longer resist the imperative to share it. It has come as an insistent spring from the depths and finds ways to flow through the human landscape whether I resist it or not. It is better to help it along than to be haunted in resistance.

When I was of middle school age I felt its first intimations. But my compeers would not receive it. All my life I have pursued world citizenship spiritually, as I now know energized by the archetype's latent expression. At last, a decade ago I wrote the book, Four Spiritualities, correlating Jungian personality typology with four parallel patterns I discerned in all branches of human religion. Surprisingly though it continues to be widely read Four Spiritualities garnered little criticism. I have received many reports of life changing recognitions. That is the word, "recognitions." In over fifty workshops, more often than not that is the response; one of the four is recognized as an underlying process in a person's spiritual journey. Affirmations have come from many religious traditions on six continents (even Antarctica). I credit these widespread "recognitions" to the existence of the Archetype of the Spirit from which Four Spiritualities springs.

In 1995 I backed into writing Four Spiritualities because I could not find it already in the literature. Alas, I am embarking likewise for Archetype of the Spirit. I have recognized a four-fold archetype manifest in the world's scriptures and religious traditions, in mythologies, in Jungian explorations of typology, symbols and motifs from the collective conscious and unconscious, in temple architecture, painting, sculpture, rituals of human religion, and in the everyday. I hope to give it expression in such a way that others will find they may enter into its powers and find it cohering and energizing their unique journeys through the joys and terrors of life.

An often heard criticism of psychological type is that it describes the dynamic processes in the human personality but does not, as is, provoke personal growth towards greater human wholeness. You may know your type preferences and the

Gnarled tree, Forbidden City, Beijing, China.

strengths and weaknesses of how you have lived your type but little is available for how to develop your uniqueness further. The discovery of the Archetype of the Spirit provides this missing resource in type literature. Growth towards human wholeness has indeed been integral in world religious culture, hidden for millennia in the shadows of ongoing spiritual traditions.

Remarkably, Carl Jung, Joseph Campbell and Micea Eliade have written extensively on the components of the Archtype of the Spirit, but never put the pieces together. I am indebted to Jung for the mandala model of human wholeness, with its quarternity, to Campbell for his extensive descriptions of the ascent of spiritual development towards enlightenment, particularly in Indian traditions, and to Eliade for his documentation world-around of practices relating to Earth, Sky, Sun, Moon and Tree.

The plan for the following six chapters follows the same order in which I discovered the Archetype of the Spirit. First through learning psychological type itself and Jung's theory, then the correlation with type of the Four Spiritualities, then the emergence of the Archetype of the Spirit through time as richly portrayed in the symbols and practices of human religion. By then I trust it will not only become radiant in your life as in mine but invite the many branches of world culture in as a friendly presence as well.

— Peter Tufts Richardson

*Oak at Avebury, England. A grove of ancient oaks overlooks the
menhir ritual circles in Avebury.*

CHAPTER ONE

UNFOLDING OF CONSCIOUSNESS

We are born in the collective. While we experience the world individually, as infants, in much of early childhood, and to a varying extent always, we interpret that experience participating in a larger body than what is defined by our skin. Pain, grief, delight and joy are experienced in the collective. As we emerge into a sense of individuality our experiences become subjective. We realize those around us, parents, siblings, society, do not have that identical original experience.[1] They can only surmise what our experience may be and we likewise can only surmise what their subjective world may be. But still we remain in large part experiencing the whole in the whole even as we are apart and aware of that portion of experience which is unique. Thus do we begin the long process of understanding our own uniqueness while monitoring those relationships in which we always participate as social animals.

It is in this search for understanding of our subjective realities, individual and collective, that we turn to psychological type or the basic functions of consciousness. As our consciousness unfolds, comes into being so that we "see" ourselves as persons in the sea of the collective, it differentiates in four aspects, two of them in a perceiving way and two of them in a judging way.[2] We have two ways of taking in information and organizing that information so that it can be further processed and prioritized. Once we know what we are experiencing we need quickly to ascertain its significance, what we make of it, how it relates to our wellbeing and activity. Thus we take in (perceive) and we act upon (form judgments about) that which we apprehend.[3] Each of us develops unique memories of experience and patterns of response to it. And from this matrix we initiate a singular and unique presence in the world.

By the time we reach adulthood we understand psychological type whether or not we have articulated its forms and definitions. We "see" the world through it and in its processes but may not have thought about the forms of our consciousness or how our consciousness flows as we live in it and through it. Most people who "learn" type experience it as a revealing of what they already know. It is archetypal, already present.

*Spring flowers,Kennebunk, Maine. For Jung, the four functions (S, N, T, F)
were the flowering of human consiousness, its differentiation.*

In our relationships to self and others the four functions form the basis for human sympathy, understanding and appreciation. Without this "language" of our conscious and unconscious processes we would be relative strangers to ourselves and others. Without a code of access to making objective its functioning we must rely on surmises far less insightful for unlocking what is actually taking place "behind the scenes."

The perceiving functions are sensing (S) and intuiting (N). The judging or "ordering" functions are thinking (T) and feeling (F). Sensing (S) has to do with apprehending what is actually there whereas intuiting (N) perceives possibilities inherent in situations and events for the future.[4] We have to know that S and N are cognizing of perception, ascertaining what it is we are experiencing: comparing it with other similar experiences (introversion) or connecting with the particular qualities inherent in the experiencing (extraversion). Thus we have two kinds of sensing and intuiting: extraverted sensing (Se) and introverted sensing (Si), extraverted intuiting (Ne) and introverted intuiting (Ni).

Let us take one example for the sensing function (S), body language. Perceiving the messages coming in from others is in large part nonverbal when we are physically present to each other. The sensing function is attuned to all the fleeting signals coming to us alongside words and silences. Extraverted sensing can immediately pick up these and quickly relay the information to the judging functions (thinking and feeling) in a constant stream of responses. If the other person is brandishing a sword this process can be so fast it seems as if the response comes right out of the experiencing itself. Extraverted sensing (Se) can be a high attunement to the present moment, in its fullness of happening. Introverted sensing (Si) takes body signals and compares them by reconstituting its store of similar signals in past experience. It is a reflecting, nuancing, process. We carry a vast universe of distinctions and qualities in our sensing function and the memories of these experiences and our judging responses to them. We often refer to these as the instinctual level of experience, the particular realm of introverted sensing (Si).

Were an intuiting type (N) to visit a broad beach of white shell sand on a bright sunny day the dazzling impact might be so overwhelming they would forget to sit down or to swim for awhile. "What if this sand were all around the city cathedral. What a dazzling taste of heaven at the temple gates! The brilliance suggests immediately enlightenment (en-light-enment), intense spiritual awareness. To walk out upon such brilliance is to be lifted, to lighten all burdens (en-lighten-ment) as if they were nothing. What wonders the world can give us, what surprises, what gifts! Heaven is present to us if we but open ourselves to it! What possibilities if only architects of the inner city could replicate this beach! Oh yes, I am on the beach, and we are going to walk on this sand." Such is a possible example of the ruminations of intuiting, in the experience of the moment itself. Such perceiving happens in a matter of seconds but even so is a slower process than sensing (particularly Se). It is as if intuiting must take what is present and converse about it, turn images into words, in order to make them real. All images have symbolic significance as well as standing for actual realities. One can see the possibilities in an experience for one's life or life in general (Ne) or connect with the archetypal significances of experience (Ni). All conscious experiences are images of significance, symbolic meanings flowing from the inherent embodied nature of experience. They are what is actually happening. With intuition what is near can be interpreted from far away, what is present can be from eternity, what is "flat" can be deep. And to "see" this way transforms experiences for the support and enrichment of life in all its possibilities.

It is the role of the judging functions, thinking (T) and feeling (F), to regulate our perceiving, sorting the vast complexity of perceptions into that with which we will deal consciously. Thinking (T) will name and categorize what comes to it and feeling (F) will give it value, ascertain what it is worth to us and to humanity in general. We perceive so much at all times that we require the judging functions to regulate that input, so that our conscious lives will not be a conveyor belt of total chaos of over stimulation. Of course the perceiving functions have already shaped (cognized) the input but the judging functions must determine what we find to have importance. Much is lost along the way. Much is put on the back burner of the unconscious. But we must be able to focus, to choose and to act.

With thinking (T) we not only have named objects and people but relational processes and systems, and how they interface, operate and develop. Thinking sorts the principles governing how things work, and the contractual arrangements of society (explicit and implicit). Who is responsible for taking care of what? What does it take to make society, an organization, a tribe or a household work? What are the logical integrities of the world and of life? Feeling (F) takes the affective input of perception and weaves it into value priorities. How should we treat each other? What kinds of qualities in relationships will build harmonies into families, associations, societies? What are the norms of behavior that we can expect of ourselves and others?

To look at an example, thinking types (T) are often found in consulting firms. Extraverted thinking (Te) might tend to pay close attention to the purpose and mission of an organization or institution, seeking out strategic leverage points and goals to spark greater efficiency or more effective efforts. If an organization is vague or fuzzy in its workings extraverted thinking (Te) will urge energetic efforts for the writing of manuals of procedure giving definition to work. Meanwhile the introverted thinking type (Ti) has been analyzing the market share of a corporation or the potential constituencies or opportunities for growth of an organization. Such analysis and interpretation can be highly original and ingenious. If a consulting client were in crisis a thinking type might propose sweeping changes, including personnel changes, more logical and hard headed than other types had been willing to entertain. Both (Te, Ti) will likely advocate knowledge and education as a route for reform and clarity for organizations and society. Should their efforts reach the end of their tether without achieving change, their frustration over the patently obvious to them may move thinking types to exit or throw up their hands in a chaos of "OK, have it your way."

To illustrate how the feeling function (F) might operate, imagine a large group in crisis over a disagreement between two prominent leaders. Both the extraverted feeling type (Fe) and the introverted feeling type (Fi) will immediately attune themselves to the rising anxiety level in the group. Assuming a level of maturity whereby they will not attempt to gloss over conflict on the one hand or become partisans in the conflict on the other hand, the extraverted feeling type (Fe) will immediately set about bringing the parties together "among friends" seeking out accord or compromise, reestablishing harmony and the group norms. At times extraverted feeling (Fe) will take on the burden of conflict as their own, fusing with it in misplaced empathy, a way extraverted feeling types burn out. The introverted feeling type (Fi) in the same situation is likely to become very quiet, fully present, reaching down to the archetypal values and calmly making them a part of the group process. If there is no response from the impass the introverted feeling type (Fi) may burst through with a prophetic voice reminding the group of its ideals and mission and how petty conflicts can sabotage them. So "out of character" are such pronouncements from the usual gentle accommodating companionship, that this may shock a group to change. The introverted feeling type will then need recovery "down time" to ease the intensity of internalization of the crisis in their inner ruminations. Feeling (Fe, Fi) resonates with the emotional states of a situation responding to them with appropriate norms and values for reestablishing social harmony and well-being for all.

It is important to keep before us that each of us lives in all eight of these function-attitudes of perceiving and judging. In any nanosecond any one of the eight may be activated. However, some will be more accessible and useable than others, while the rest will be loose and relatively unformed. Jung was the first to point out that the personality will be led by a superior function which has differentiated furthest in consciousness and that most of the remaining functions will be largely reconstellated in the unconscious. To the degree a function is conscious to that degree will it be differentiated enough to be a reliable process. We come to prefer it as a known quantity guiding our responses to life. This superior or dominant function can be either perceiving or judging in either extraverted or introverted attitude. A second function, called the auxiliary function, will complement the dominant function assisting it with a balancing requirement. If the dominant is perceiving the auxiliary will be judging and if the dominant is extraverted the auxiliary will be introverted. Likewise if the dominant is judging the auxiliary will be perceiving and if the dominant is introverted the auxiliary will be extraverted. Thus psychological type describes the underlying processes of consciousness, our preferences for perceiving (P) or judging (J), and for extraverting or introverting, which lead and which are in a supporting role, and which are more or less differentiated into consciousness and thus readily and reliably accessible when needed.

A popular instrument for assisting us to identify which of these processes are prominent in our personal psychology is the Myers Briggs Type Indicator (MBTI™). Created by Isabel Briggs-Myers in 1943 and developed by many others since, the Indicator helps us to identify the dominant and auxiliary functions in their attitudes, extraversion (E) or Introversion (I). In addition the MBTI™ adds a second polarity of attitudes indicating how a person relates to the surrounding world, primarily with the perceiving function (P) in their type or the judging function (J) in their type. Thus an extraverted person would interact with the world around them primarily with their dominant function while the introverted type would relate primarily through their auxiliary function. There are sixteen different psychological types, or sixteen ways of identifying the underlying processes of human personality[5] (see FIGURE 1).

ESTP	Extraverted Sensing	with	Introverted Thinking
ESFP	Extraverted Sensing	with	Introverted Feeling
ISTJ	Introverted Sensing	with	Extraverted Thinking
ISFJ	Introverted Sensing	with	Extraverted Feeling
ESTJ	Extraverted Thinking	with	Introverted Sensing
ENTJ	Extraverted Thinking	with	Introverted Intuition
ISTP	Introverted Thinking	with	Extraverted Sensing
INTP	Introverted Thinking	with	Extraverted Intuition
ESFJ	Extraverted Feeling	with	Introverted Sensing
ENFJ	Extraverted Feeling	with	Introverted Intuition
ISFP	Introverted Feeling	with	Extraverted Sensing
INFP	Introverted Feeling	with	Extraverted Intuition
ENFP	Extraverted Intuition	with	Introverted Feeling
ENTP	Extraverted Intuition	with	Introverted Thinking
INFJ	Introverted Intuition	with	Extraverted Feeling
INTJ	Introverted Intuition	with	Extraverted Thinking

FIGURE 1 Sixteen Types

In 1923 with the publishing of his *Psychological Types*, Carl Jung arranged the four functions in a compass[6] (see FIGURE 2). To have sensing (S) and intuiting (N) opposite each other and thinking (T) and feeling (F) in opposition across the circle emphasizes the central principle of polarity. Opposition is critical for understanding the workings of psychological type for when one function is energized its opposite is in shadow. We rely on our preferences (relatively differentiated into consciousness) more than upon their opposites (relatively hidden in the unconscious) even after we have matured enough to call upon the non preferred functions as situations warrant. The built-in oppositions energize the psyche and the preferred functions give the personality conscious direction and, if well developed, a natural efficiency.

Jung also speaks of the function pairs, for all of us must depend upon both perceiving and judging and must be able to enter into both extraversion and introversion.[7] Jungian analyst, John Giannini, has recently emphasized that the "couplings" or function pairs can also be fruitfully studied in their oppositions.[8] If we rotate Jung's compass 45° we can preserve oppositions of both the single and the paired functions bringing the latter to increased prominence (see FIGURE 3).

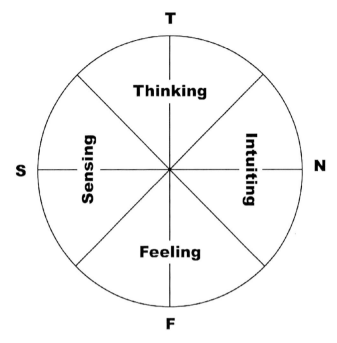

FIGURE 2 Functions Compass

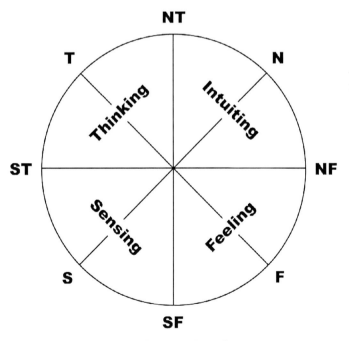

FIGURE 3 Function Pairs Compass

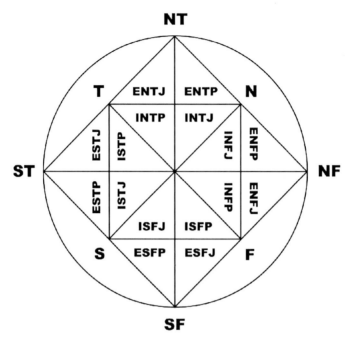

FIGURE 4 Sixteen Types Compass

From a compass with the function pairs it is only a short step to showing the relationships of all sixteen types in a compass or mandala form.[9] In 1996 I published what I call the Four Spiritualities Mandala (see FIGURE 4). This figure shows the sixteen types in their dynamic relationships without reductively placing them into boxes. The polarities, central in Jungian theory, are clearly emphasized for individual and function pairs as well as between types across the circle. As mandalas are meant for individual reflection we have here a model of human wholeness in both its individual (compensatory) and its collective (complementarity of types) forms. All the dominant sensing, intuiting, thinking and feeling types are clustered in groups of four across from their opposing types. Each type is across the circle from their opposite type. For example, ISTJ is opposite ENFP and INFP is opposite ESTJ. Types opposite in their function attitudes are hinged to each other, for example, ESFJ is hinged to ISFP showing the two attitudes of the feeling function as do ENFJ and INFP. It is this energizing dynamics in type that gives the Jungian model of the differentiation of consciousness its importance as "the basis for a critical psychology."[10] Leola Haas and Mark Henziler[11] have pointed out that type opposition is most complete with the same attitudes and opposite functions, for example INTJ vs. ISFJ or ENFJ vs. ESTJ. This pattern can be readily seen across the type compass.

Clinical psychologist, Naomi Quenk, and Jungian analyst, John Beebe, have given special attention to the fourth or inferior function. For example if a person has a dominant extraverted thinking (Te) the inferior will be introverted feeling (Fi). Being in opposition the inferior function can be either in conflict with or appear numinous to the dominant function. Quenk has drawn attention to the inferior as a "doorway to the unconscious."[12] In her extensive work she has detailed how for each type when a person is overwhelmed or stressed out by circumstances in their lives the dominant will temporarily drop into shadow. The inferior will assume a guiding hand but being relatively undifferentiated and largely unconscious, will do so in a rather chaotic manner. A person will seem "beside themselves." It is best to let such episodes run their course until the personality rights itself into balance with the dominant "in charge." We can learn from these eruptions of the inferior, differentiating this function a bit further and gaining insight into the compensating energies in the unconscious.

John Beebe stresses the fourth function as numinous.[13] The dominant in consciousness may find the inferior function strangely and mysteriously attractive, a kind of siren call reminding it of its own limitations as part of the larger self. He gives the inferior function the archetype of the anima/animus, that mysterious figure that comes to us in dreams or when we least expect it in our waking hours, reminding us of the great creativity inherent in the presence of the dominant in consciousness versus a great void mostly hidden which if it could be revealed (differentiated) into consciousness could be a powerful balancing energy in our quest for wholeness. The inferior can haunt us, even torment us, if it is ignored. It is a kind of fatal attraction for we usually don't know what to do with it when it is constellated, even momentarily. According to Beebe our glimpses of the inferior function are helpful in ascertaining our dominant function and whether it is in balance with other aspects of the self. We can find great learning there and if we can differentiate even some, great added power and resourcefulness.

Beebe arranges all eight of the function-attitudes of each type along a spine, from the dominant, through the inferior and then to the remaining four function-attitudes which will be almost if not wholly in the unconscious.[14] And for each of the eight he assigns an archetype which characterizes its part in the whole. These archetypes for each of the function attitudes, from dominant to eighth, are: hero/heroine, parent, child or puer, anima/animus, opposing personality, witch/senex, trickster, and demonic/angelic.

There are those who can occasionally sense the presence of an activated archetype in some way making its presence felt from the unconscious but for most of us most of the time such an eruption will be too subtle for our recognition. Nevertheless they are impacting our personal emotional states, moods, perspectives

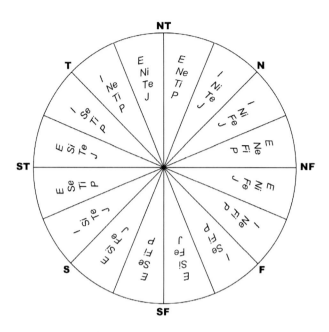

FIGURE 5A Function Attitudes Wheel

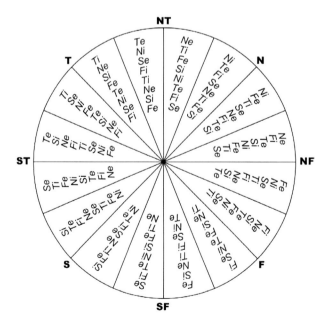

FIGURE 5B Function Attitudes Wheel

and even decisions throughout our lives. To find your eight function-attitudes find your type on the modified mandala (FIGURE 5A) and then in the second compass find the order for the eight function-attitudes for your type (FIGURE 5B).

For example, for an ESTP the sequence down along the spine would be:
1. Se   will be in the hero archetype
2. Ti   will be in the parent archetype
3. Fe   will be in the child or puer archetype
4. Ni   will be in the anima/animus archetype
5. Si   will be in the opposing personality
6. Te   will be in the witch/senex archetype
7. Fi   will be in the trickster archetype
8. Ne   will be in the demonic or angelic archetype

As can be seen in only this brief introduction to type it is a rich language for exploration of the nature we all share. It is meant to remain fluid, identifying underlying processes in the psyche without rigid deterministic conclusions. Type theory for example may explain a preference but not predict how competent a person will be in living that preference. Type theory is not predictive of success or failure. It does not render imperatives such that we can say a person ought to pursue a certain vocation or will hold certain political or theological beliefs. It is important to focus upon type as revealing how a person responds to life but always as processes within a larger narrative and content of their life story. It is understandable that in a century marked by behaviorism and trait theories in academia, attempts would be made to impose them on type theory. They are incompatible as psychological type is part of a larger dynamic theory of the self developed by Carl Jung. So too in an age of public relations and a consumer economy it could be predicted that attempts would be made to accommodate the theory to the needs of a huckstering society. The strength of psychological type as an explanation of the differentiation of human consciousness is shown in that it has maintained intact the integrity of its theory and even experienced a lively enrichment of its principles.

However, it is important to caution all individuals meeting the theory for the first time: learning the four letters of your type is only the beginning. If with taking the MBTI™ and undergoing the self selecting and verification process you now have your four letters, the journey of self discovery is only beginning.[15] I urge a further exploration particularly as the quest for wholeness individually must be seen in the context of the collective wholeness which includes all sixteen types in a larger narrative of the spiritual emergence of humanity on this planet. It is to this story that we now turn.

Floor grate design, The Cathedral Basillica of St.Francis of Assisi, Santa Fe, NM

Solar sheild with quarternity, symbol of the "people of the sun", Palatki Ruins, near Sedona, AZ

Sandstone cliff formation at Palatki Ruins, near Sedona, AZ.

CHAPTER TWO

Setting the Stage————————

It is one thing to assert the presence of an archetype and quite another to prove it. An archetype must be universal. It must be present, either latent or manifest, in every life, in every place, in every time. Most of our human emergence on the planet was lived before the invention of alphabets, written scriptures or literatures. Our spiritual origins are carved in wood and stone and present within us in the very structures of our humanity.

According to Carl Jung "archetypes are, by definition, factors and motifs that arrange the psychic elements into certain images, characterized as archetypal, but in such a way that they can be recognized only from the effects they produce. They exist pre-consciously."[1] They are primordial images from the unconscious. Like a fish at the water's surface, an archetype swims by and if we do not attend to it, it returns to the depths, its energy increases and reappears. If we do not catch it, the presence in the depths continues a life of its own swimming in the unconscious. It may erupt into consciousness as a complex and throw our lives into imbalance or disarray. If still unattended it may fade from awareness, but be felt in various ways as an absence causing degrees of ennui, a draining of meaning, increasing chaos or moodiness.

There are many archetypes: the mother and father archetypes, the child or puer, the hero, the parent, the warrior or king/queen, the witch/senex, the trickster, the demonic, the anima/animus, even god/goddess archetypes. Jung added certain structures as archetypes such as the Self or Psyche, shadow, the mandala and type functions on a compass with sensation, intuition, thinking and feeling. Archetypes activated in the course of a lifetime ask to be resolved and assimilated into the fabric of our ongoing consciousness. We will miss opportunities when we are called to this task but we dare not miss too many! Of the many archetypes none can be more central than the archetype of our spiritual origins. While not the only one with spiritual significance, the Archetype of the Spirit is central. Like the others it is present within us whether we unlock its powers or not.

Archetypes have a way of coming to the surface when provoked in life crises or social turmoil. When we tap into our spiritual resources for comfort, for meaning or wisdom, or for explanation, the archetype will manifest in dreams, or in motifs expressed by society's artists, poets, prophets in the collective. Seldom are these expressions 'pure' as in a blueprint. Rather they take on local forms and narratives. But when the archetype is experienced and understood, such expressions can be recognized and read as a universal language of our spirituality.

Jungian analyst, Angelo Spoto, emphasizes there are certain times in the life cycle when an archetypal eruption is likely to confront us, particularly at midlife, when the dominant function is so triumphant that life becomes flat. Out of the routine of boredom a certain restlessness sets in.[2] Buddhists call it duhkha, or a pervasive unsatisfactoriness of life, a free floating suffering.[3] At midlife we ask, "is this it? Is there nothing more to life than perpetuating this?"[4] A person can be riding a peak of success at work and in civic life. A person could have achieved all the accoutrements of the "good life" as beamed in the daily smiling and vibrant faces of television ads. Or failure thus far could haunt a person who wonders if their life is going anywhere. This spiritual crisis has been called the dark night of the soul among Christian mystics. It is at this point of opportunity that a person may experience dreams full of serpents calling them to a new beginning, creative enterprise, renewal. Or the contrasexual image of the anima/animus may appear reminding us that there are major aspects of self neglected by the dominance of an ego stability, energized by the need for balance and development. Such experiences and images are archetypal from the shadows of the unconscious.

> The archetypes of the collective unconscious…precipitate complexes of ideas in the form of mythological motifs. They are spontaneous phenomena which are not subject to our will.[5]

To experience their presence is the beginning of new life.

To set the stage it is essential to outline the relationship of psychological type to the model of Four Spiritualities and through to the archetype which gave birth to them. We will do this through an exploration of the mandala image of the archetype. In the following chapter is an outline description of Four Spiritualities before we develop an historical account of the archetype's emergence in human culture and contemporary experience in the three following chapters.

In my earlier book, Four Spiritualities, I described four parallel patterns found in local religious practices universally around the planet. And when I learned of Jungian personality typology I quickly recognized how completely these four spiritualities correlated with type. I should not have been surprised as spirituality resides at the deepest levels of our human consciousness constantly replenished and enriched from the unconscious. And it sorts into four patterns of differentiation. We can therefore place the sixteen types into a Jungian compass form I call the Four Spiritualities Mandala as described in Chapter One (see FIGURE 6). It is the purpose of this book to document and show the dynamics of this Mandala as an archetype of human spiritual origins.

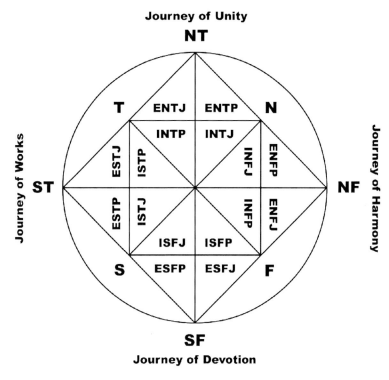

FIGURE 6 Four Spiritualities Mandala

The Archetype of the Spirit or a model of human wholeness, and the Four Spiritualities Mandala which derives from it, can be represented with the universal forms of the circle, the square and the cross. One of the great ritual centers of the world for example is the Altar of Heaven in Beijing where all three forms come together.[6]

The circle is the symbol of sky or the cosmic dimension of life. Since earliest times we have gazed out at the ordered patterns of the stars and motions of the planets, the mathematical regularity of their cycles. It has long been thought that if we could regulate our lives as well as sky perhaps a benign and supportive moral order might be established. But of course from the sky comes lightning and thunder, tornados and hurricanes, asteroids and a sense of mysteries and powers beyond human control. Perhaps they can be placated, perhaps we can gain a more complete knowledge and understanding for our human destinies.

The square is a universal symbol of earth coming into usage very early when earth was perceived as a flat plain with four corners or a land island surrounded by waters.[7] And of course in China "the Middle Kingdom" was at its center. When the empire was well governed harvests were abundant, the people prospered and the "mandate of heaven" was assured.[8] The dome of sky and the kingdom were in accord. We can say the square is like a pedestal forming the base upon which all else in our lives rests.

Huan Qui Tan at Tian Tan or Altar of Heaven, Beijing, China. Notice the context of the square (earth) and the circle (cosmos) with the raised altar itself in the foreground. Procession walkways radiate out to the compass points with elegant gateways creating a magnificent quarternity.

The cross transmits energy from the center of the earth towards the four cardinal points and brings energy from these opposing points towards the center. At the center is the axis of the world, the sacred mountain, or the tree of life. The tree of life sustains us all. An instance of sublime paradox was the crucifixion of Christ on this same tree,[9] a warning for us that this powerful mandala and archetype is not necessarily "nice." It is real.

Jung was the first in the emergence of Western psychology to recognize that the mandala is archetypal, the image of human wholeness. In a discussion of quarternity (a circle divided into four parts by a cross) Jung mentioned it signified the Deity or tetrakty (father, son, holy ghost, Mary).[10] He also believed it is the image of the unconscious mind.

The squared circle, a circle within a square (or vice versa) brings earth (square) and heaven (circle) together, "the pneumatic deity" and the goddess.[11]

> Creation begins with an act of division of the opposites that are united in the deity. From their splitting arises, in a gigantic explosion of energy, the multiplicity of the world.

He continues relating the larger world to the psyche itself:

Obelisk from Heliopolis, Cairo, Egypt, brought to Rome in 37 A.D. and eventually set up in St. Peter's Piazza. This solar symbol acts as the axis in a mandala featuring the circle and cross but not the square (earth).

There are innumerable variants of the motif . . . but they are all based on the squaring of a circle. Their basic motif is the premonition of a centre of personality, a kind of central point within the psyche to which everything is related . . . The energy of the central point is manifested in the almost irresistible compulsion and urge to become what one is. . .[12]

I have learned in the process of relating personality theory to the larger corpus of Jungian psychology that to focus upon personality (as in the MBTI™) alone relegates the archetype to oneself. To focus rather on the archetype of human wholeness, the Self as mediated by the conscious personality (manifest in the Four Spiritualities Mandala) directly, brings us into participation in the human family. We are a part of the whole and the whole is within us all. Each of us functions as but one of the sixteen possible types, surrounded by near neighbors and other types in opposition positions either antagonistic or numinous. Mandalas are drawn for reflective spiritual practice, to relate the parts to the whole or the individual to the collective. A contemplation of the Four Spiritualities Mandala (FIGURE 6) reviews for us the unique qualities of all sixteen components, their near and far relationships to each other and the dynamic forces inherent in the complementarity of types, We may increasingly activate parts of ourselves latent but overlooked until awakened in the course of this practice.

There is a larger picture beyond the individual in the collective. During most of human history spirituality could not be contained in written scriptures, canons or theological treatises spelling out beliefs, doctrines, philosophies or received opinions. Alphabets and writing had not been invented. Instead on temple walls, in shrines in the home, in drawings in the sand at tribal gatherings a model of human wholeness was in a mandala known to all. Images and motifs could be referenced with symbols readily at hand: earth, sky, sun and moon, drawn on a circle at the cardinal compass points with the tree of life or human spine drawn through the center as a key for spiritual development. Variations of this Archetype of the Spirit were drawn as mandalas everywhere humans are found on the globe.

Jain mandala with an ahimsa theme, bronze from South India.
Note its square (earth) form with a solar center, from the author's collection.

In the more archaic form the circle (sky) is placed to the north and the square (earth) is placed to the south forming a primary polarity. Sun, a double circle, is in the west and moon, a crescent, is placed in the east, forming a secondary polarity. A spine of the primary polarity is entwined by two serpents, symbolic of creative growth or healing as in the caduceus (see FIGURE 7).

A mandala has traditionally been the means for focusing the mind, all we know or imagine of life, into a single orientation and meditation. From this practice we form a coherent balance to guide our journey. A spiritual orientation must be at once omni-directional and centered, while always adapting to the exigencies of each day, moving in the flowing emergence of the great story. After describing the Four Spiritualities of human nature we will explore the presence through time of the underlying Archetype of the Spirit, showing its motifs in more detail around the world, diving into its dynamics as it has been and is lived in our uniquely personal spiritual narratives.

But first a note on "Spirituality" a most slippery word in our language which merits some definition. Often contrasted with "religion" I characterize it as both

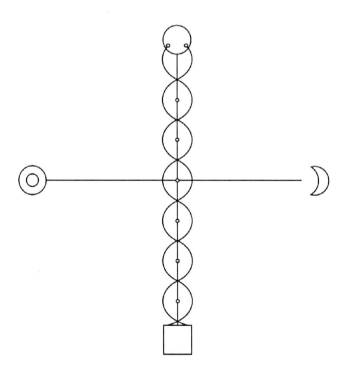

FIGURE 7 Archtype of the Spirit

larger and more particularly focused than religion. We can speak of our humanity in a universal way as the spiritual presence on this planet. In this planetary sense we are all kinsfolk in one spiritual emergence. Religion characterizes the local social forms of our human spirituality. As social beings we congregate in religious networks for celebration of our human condition and in mutual support and comfort for life's journey. To abdicate our presence in religious congregations removes us from this cohering social responsibility and blunts access by others to what we may have learned from our own spiritual journey (and access by us to theirs). Spirituality is an individual journey as each of us individuates in our uniqueness, contributes our part in the whole and in the face of our mortality aspires to live with spiritual poise. We only can experience our birth and our death. Thus spirituality and religion are modulations of but one essential reality in our lives.

Often confused with specific beliefs, rituals or practices, spirituality is rather attraction to a numinous reality larger than ourselves. Such a reality is a locus of purpose or meaning or human values. It can involve either theistic or naturalistic perspectives. In meaning it is cosmic in orientation, in power personal, in relationship social. There are emotional tones but it is not emotional states only, there are intellectual qualities but it is not an exercise of intellect only, there are ethical imperatives but it is not a call to justice only, there are practices associated with it but it cannot be attained through disciplines only, there are mystic attunements but it is not "proved" by interpretations of mystic experience only. Described as a foundation of all else, the "ground of being," embodied, compatible with deeper levels of Jung's Self, it represents an intensification, a gathering in human wholeness, the deepest longing for connection in our natures.

Our spirituality is not something we invent but rather is a presence in our lives, individually and collectively. We may access it at any time in any place on the planet. It is a process of human recognition of the best that is in us, a process of invocation which comes from within, which we can feel as present to us in the most local or the most universal context in which we live and move and have our existence. Spirituality IS, but it also grows within us, like leaven forming a loaf of bread. A purpose in our lives is to make what IS conscious in our living. Each growth spurt throws us into imbalance if not panic for spirituality inherently presents us a challenge to grow in our uniqueness, to become whole by differentiating those aspects of ourselves which define our full humanity. Not only do we live, reflectively and expressively in our strengths, finding our unique contribution for the life around us, but we have latent within us the full range of our humanity.

To embark upon a quest for spiritual wholeness requires that we recognize its difficulty, its risks, even the possibility of shipwreck. Balance in the journey requires episodes of imbalance, even chaos. For every insight gained there will be myriad

Medallion, part of décor of Al-Rafai Mosque, Cairo. At the center is the heart chakra but the whole has a sky bias, to be anticipated in Islamic culture.

influences unfathomed below the surface of the sea our small vessel so tentatively sails. In the words of Carl Jung:

> The right way to wholeness is made up, unfortunately, of fateful detours and wrong turnings. It is a longissima via, not straight but snakelike, a path that unites the opposites in the manner of the guiding caduceus, a path whose labyrinthine twists and turns are not lacking in terrors.[13]

Indeed, the stakes are high but as far as we know we have only one lifetime to bring our unique experiment into its own destiny.

It is in this context of balance and wholeness that we come to the switchboard of spirituality, namely the human personality, to which we now turn.

Paleolithic limestone screen with four spirals in relief with pitted background, from the Middle Temple at Tarxien, National Museum in Valletta, Malta.

CHAPTER THREE

FOUR SPIRITUALITIES

Four Spiritualities and the Archetype of the Spirit I believe to be mutually reinforcing and continuous. The four journeys, Unity (NT), Devotion (SF), Works (ST), and Harmony (NF), are to be found in all of us, in differing strengths and with one leading. A large part of spiritual development is bringing each and all into an integration and dynamic balance in consciousness and the self. Antagonism toward any or an absence of one or two immediately raises a red flag for early work in the journey. The Four Spiritualities Mandala, (below) shows the relationships of each of the MBTI™ types to the other fifteen and the four spiritualities in their polar and adjacent relationships, a model for human wholeness.

In a critical sense it is less important to know your individual type than it is to know your-type-in-relationship with each and all others. It is more important to live in the whole, the mandala of human wholeness, than to live apart and isolated. To perceive oneself as active in the whole, the whole emotional, relational body of humanity is the essential lesson of life. It completes the cycle from infancy to mature adulthood or elderhood. Coming to understand the mandala of human wholeness marks the achievement of participation in the body of humanity.

It is in this awareness, this imperative, that we consider the four spiritualities. We discover that one of the four characterizes the manner of our journey, the qualities of our responses to life and our contributions to the whole. All four are in us, a part of us in our experience of life. Therefore we will resonate with all four spiritualities. Without the prominence of one with the presence of the other three it would be difficult to awaken our human sympathies when we must respond to the needs and aspirations of others while leading with our own unique and we hope competent journey.

I. Journey of Unity

The Journey of Unity carrying the sky archetype, intuitive thinking (NT), has several characteristic qualities, summarized by the words: principles, truth, clarity and justice.

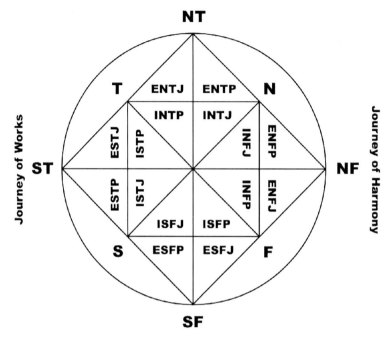

FOUR SPIRITUALITIES MANDALA

The Journey of Unity is a pilgrimage to discover the great organizing principles of the universe, of society, of life. The Buddha discovered the Four Noble Truths after years of failure. Under the Bodhi Tree he discovered the principle, duhkha, suffering, the pervasive unsatisfactoriness of life, all of us sooner or later encounter. Albert Schweitzer discovered his great ethical principle, "reverence for life," after years of struggle. He discovered it watching a herd of hippopotamuses in a river in Africa. In his words (found in his Autobiography):

> Lost in thought I sat on the deck of the barge, struggling to find the elementary and universal conception of the ethical which I had not discovered in any philosophy. Sheet after sheet I covered with disconnected sentences, merely to keep myself concentrated on the problem. Late on the third day, at the very moment when, at sunset, we were making our way through a herd of hippopotamuses, there flashed upon my mind, unforeseen and unsought, the phrase, "Reverence for Life." The iron door had yielded: the path in the thicket had become visible. Now I had found my way to the idea in

The Buddha, bronze at Patna Museum, Bihar Province, India. Buddha's position is a counterclockwise touching of earth while receiving of sky. Halo is a solar motif.

Margaret Fuller, a leading nineteenth century American Transcendentalist. Like the Buddha, and her grand-nephew, R. Buckminster Fuller, in her writings she gives us examples of NT or sky spirituality.

R. Buckminster Fuller, August 1977, First Parish, Kennebunk, ME. Note the intuitive embrace of universe. Photograph by Isabel Lewando, York County Coast Star

William Ellery Channing, Unitarian Theologian in Boston (1780-1842).

Thursday

Dear Pete & Eleanor,

Loved your Easter sermon. Always thought the Lillies of the field was stupid and bad advice. I still think it is as it stands. However, your enterpretation I liked. To bad it isn't in there.

The young man advised to sell all and become a pauper also was bad advise. What do you say about that? There must be more to the story that we aren't aware of! — As you see I don't like loose ends!

Keep them coming Eleanor. Would so much like to see you. Lots to catch up on!

Love to both

Moms.

Letter to author from his mother, April 1996, on a sermon with the text,
Matthew 6:25-34. She was an ENTP writing to an INFP.

which affirmation of the world and ethics are contained side by
side. Now I knew that the ethical acceptance of the world and of
life, together with the ideals of civilization contained in this
concept, has a foundation in thought.[1]

It was important to Schweitzer that thought be the basis knitting together both a
world view and an ethic in one unifying principle.

Those on the Journey of Unity, are in a constant search for truth. In the words of
the *Bhagavad Gita*:

When ignorance is destroyed by knowledge of the self, then, like
the sun, knowledge illumines ultimate reality.[2]

Margaret Fuller said of truth:

Truth is the nursing mother of genius. No man can be absolutely
true to himself, eschewing cant, compromise, servile imitation, and
complaisance, without becoming original, for there is in every
creature a fountain of life which, if not choked back by stones and
other dead rubbish, will create a fresh atmosphere and bring life to
fresh beauty. . .

. . .the spirit of truth, purely worshipped, shall turn our acts and
forbearances alike to profit, informing them with oracles which the
latest time shall bless.[3]

Boston theologian, William Ellery Channing, gives us an example of how at
times an NT will take hold of NF values and give them expression as NT truths.

That unbounded spiritual energy which we call God, is conceived
by us only through consciousness, through the knowledge of
ourselves . . . The Infinite Light would be forever hidden from us,
did not kindred rays dawn and brighten within us. God is another
name for human intelligence raised above all error and
imperfection, and extended to all possible truth. The same is true of
God's goodness. How do we understand this, but by the principle of
love implanted in the human breast? . . . Men, as by a natural
inspiration, have agreed to speak of conscience as the voice of God,
as the Divinity within us . . . the universe, I know, is full of God.[4]

The Journey of Unity strives for clarity as a mystic goal of the spiritual life. Buckminster Fuller said of this clarity:

> It consists in an intuitive, non-graphable awareness of perfection, or of unity, or of eternity, or of infinity or of truth.[5]

In the *Dhammapada*:

> Clear thinking leads to Nirvana, a confused mind is a place of death. Clear thinkers do not die, the confused ones have never lived. The wise [person] appreciates clear thinking, delights in its purity, and selects it as the means to Nirvana.[6]

Thomas Merton when he first experienced this sense of clarity in a Trappist monastery knew that he had come home.

> The embrace of it, the silence! . . . spoke to me, and spoke louder and more eloquently than any voice and in the middle of that quiet, clean smelling room, with the moon pouring its peacefulness in through the open window, . . . I realized truly whose house that was, O glorious Mother of God![7]

The ethical expression for those on the Journey of Unity, is social justice as an important aspect of their spirituality. The prophet Amos is famous for the words:

> I despise your feasts and I take no delight in your solemn assemblies. . . Take away from me the noise of your songs; to the melody of your harps I will not listen. But let justice roll down like waters, and righteousness like an everflowing stream.[8]

Amos had opinions and people found him irritating. Particularly offensive to his SF hearers was his condemnation of beloved devotional practices. After his first sermon they sent him back to hewing his sycamore trees.

Theodore Parker contrasted what he called "remedial Justice" with "palliative Charity." Again we see the contrast of "remedial Justice" (NT) with "palliative Charity" (SF). He would not have held much patience with soup kitchens and food pantries. Rather he would turn society upside down so that everyone would have work, food, clothing, shelter, basic human dignity, "remedial Justice."[9]

II. Journey of Devotion

The polar opposite of the Journey of Unity is the Journey of Devotion, carrying the earth archetype, sensing feeling (SF).

Whereas the Journey of Unity enjoys the big picture, the limitless horizons, dispassionate global possibilities, this spirituality, the Journey of Devotion, loves the immediate and direct, the here and now, "acting locally" rather than "thinking globally." The Journey of Devotion concentrates on religion as intensely personal, as acts of piety, direct experience and service.

Characteristically Devotion is intensely personal. Ramakrishna, the great Hindu saint, invoked the goddess Kali:

> O Mother, make me mad with Thy love! What need have I of knowledge or reason? . . . There is no need for much reading of the scriptures. You would be inclined to argue and debate. What you gain by repeating the Name of God with love ten times is the very essence of the Scriptures. Be mad for God, truly be athirst for God, the Divine Intoxication. Love . . . opens all doors.[10]

When Sarah Flower Adams wrote "Nearer My God to Thee" she was not referring to some far-off abstract impersonal deity which perhaps is running the universe. She is addressing "My God," a personal god she is intimately acquainted with. At the time of her approaching death she feels "nearer, my God, to thee."[11]

The Journey of Devotion, engages in acts of piety, hands on, tangible, real, in the here and now. The candles are lit in bright and polished candlesticks, incense is burning, bells sound, beautifully hand embroidered vestments are worn, the flowers are arranged gloriously on the altar.

My wife, Eleanor, and I visited a number of goddess temples in Malta where a Paleolithic people had arranged megalithic stones with such precision and grace that several thousand years later, not even a razor blade would fit between them; huge stones arranged like flowers.

Mohammed lived profoundly a life in the Journey of Devotion. His ministry was intensely personal and tangible. He speaks of his own life under the care of Allah in the *Qur'an*:

Saivite priest, at the fountain beneath the goddess Karveri Mater, a consort of Shiva. Priest assists worshipers properly placing offerings at the Lingam/Yoni, handing out flowers and anointing with an oil paste.

Sculpture of St. Antonio, Franciscan Monastery, courtyard of the Basilica di Sant' Apollinare Nuovo, Ravenna, Italy. The sensing feeling, earth orientation of St. Francis himself has remained strong in his order.

Buddhist devotion at the Lama Temple, Beijing, China.

Did he not find thee
An orphan and give thee
Shelter (and care)?

And he found thee
Wandering, and He gave
Thee guidance.

And he found thee
In need, and made
Thee independent.[12]

Mohammed created the five requirements of all who follow Islam: to recite the Shahada, "There is no God but Allah, and Mohammed is his Prophet;"[13] to do prescribed prayer rituals every day; to give alms to widows, orphans, strangers and the poor, to fast in the month of Ramadan; and to make a pilgrimage to Mecca. What Mohammed said about alms giving is the essence of the Journey of Devotion:

The best of almsgiving is that which springeth from the heart, and is uttered by the lips to soften the wounds of the injured.[14]

The Journey of Devotion is based in direct personal experience. St. Francis entered the Chapel of San Damiano, a little abandoned church beside the road. He knelt before the dusty altar and suddenly heard a voice: "Go, Francis, and repair my falling house!" He took this revelation literally as SFs have been known to do and spent years traveling around repairing abandoned churches.

In the story of Martha and Mary in *Luke*, the women are on the Journey of Devotion, Martha serving the guests, Mary anointing the feet of Jesus with oil.[15]

In ethical expression the Journey of Devotion, engages in direct service to others, hands on, immediate and caring response to real and present human hurts, and pain, and need. Mother Teresa is a quintessential example of the Journey of Devotion and said:

Love has to be put into action and that action is service.[16]

My favorite Christmas story is Van Dyke's, The Story of the Other Wise Man, the fourth wise man who didn't get to the manger because he stopped to help a sick man along the way. There is nothing complex in the work of Nicodemus, the giving of alms, the acts of mercy of the goddess, Kuan Yin, the touching of the lepers by the healing hands of St. Francis. It is true devotion in serving others.

Mahatma Gandhi, a man of action, sensing thinking, solar spirituality. Sculpture at Visva-Bharati, Shantiniketan, West Bengal, India.

III. Journey of Works

The Journey of Works carries the archetype of the sun, sensing thinking (ST). Its characteristics include submission to a covenant relationship, need for clear cut identity, focus on our life's work itself, and stewardship.

The world and society needs to be an orderly place, where we live in covenant with each other and with life, where we know what is expected of us, what our duty is in the whole picture. There are important covenants in religion, the Code of Hammurabi, the Ten Commandments, the Laws of Manu, the Sharia tradition in Islam, Roman Catholic or Anglican canon law. Even less exacting expectations are clear in their guidance with a balance of reciprocity.

> Whatever you wish that [others] would do to you, do so to them.
> You shall love your neighbor as yourself.
> And forgive us our debts, as we also have forgiven our debtors.[17]

In the Anglican *Book of Common Prayer* is an important statement of confession:

> . . . We have offended against thy holy laws. We have left undone those things which we ought to have done, And we have done those things which we ought not to have done.[18]

Edward Everett Hale, a Unitarian minister in Boston for over 60 years, and chaplain of the U.S. Senate, wrote:

> This true allegiance of man to the Infinite Law implies and involves more than verbal truth. It is the obedience of every act, so that the man does without concealment, without pretense, without exaggeration, the thing he undertakes to do. The errand boy does not loiter on his errand. The sentinel never misses a turn of his round. The screw-maker never puts one deficient screw in the parcel. We shall gain this absolute allegiance when the kingdom of God wholly comes. To gain it, to bring in that kingdom, is our present hope and duty.[19]

Look up and not down:
Look forward and not back;
Look out and not in—
Lend a Hand!

Edward E Hale

Statue of Edward Everett Hale, Unitarian minister in Boston's
Back Bay, can be found today in the Boston Public Garden,
well known for founding his Lend A Hand clubs, a
part of his sensing thinking, solar, spirituality.

Hale organized Lend a Hand Clubs and Look Up Legions with the motto:

> Look up and not down.
> Look forward and not back.
> look out and not in.
> Lend a hand![20]

Here is a classic (ESTJ)"boots and saddles," do your part, pull your share of the load, summary of our covenant one with another.

In the *Bhagavad Gita*, Krishna says to Arjuna:

> These worlds would collapse if I did not perform action; I would create disorder in society, living beings would be destroyed.[21]

The work of each one of us, each doing our part in our own sphere, keeps the chaos away and brings in the order.

Those on the Journey of Works like to have things spelled out, a clear cut identity for themselves and for the groups that hold their commitment. They like congregational mission statements that aren't too vague and mushy. Martin Luther was unambiguous about his identity in a speech at the Diet of Worms:

> . . . my conscience is captive to the Word of God. I cannot and I will not recant anything, for to go against conscience is neither right nor safe. Here I stand. I cannot do otherwise. God help me.
> Amen.[22]

From this sense of strong identity, and belief in the authority and destiny of the right, we find the largest vision of the Journey of Works. Julia Ward Howe, penned perhaps the most stirring ST hymn for all time:

> Mine eyes have seen the glory
>   of the coming of the Lord;
> He is trampling out the vintage
>   where the grapes of wrath are stored.[23]

The Journey of Works focuses upon work itself as spiritual practice. Brother Lawrence, a Carmelite monk, carried on a dialog with God through the daily work of his kitchen, what he called "The Practice of the Presence of God."[24] A former

Apricot Altar, constructed in the apricot grove
where Confucius taught with his students,
Qu Fu, China. This grove is a
portion of a major Confucian temple
complex in Confucius' home town.

Tomb stone of Confucius, Qu Fu, China.

parishioner of mine, walked to work at his insurance office on Main Street every working day of his life until he died in his late 80's. He always had a smile. As long as he sat at his desk on Main Street, it was the same, stable, dependable, friendly town it was supposed to be. All was well. According to Mahatma Gandhi, work itself can be a means of self transcendence. He says:

> This world suffers bondage from work unless it is work done as yajna . . . In other words, any work dedicated to God helps one to attain [release].[25]

Those on the Journey of Works, hold a responsible stewardship towards human institutions and resources and stewardship towards the natural world. When one of his disciples asked Confucius what he would do first if he were running the world, he answered, "the rectification of names." In other words, know what words actually mean, make sure everyone knows what you mean when you set out in order to make life fair, equitable, ordered by all.

In its more sublime levels in the Confucian Journey of Works, the poet, Po Chü I, wrote about a householder who bought a new house and moved his family to it because in the courtyard was a beautiful stand of pine trees. Then after years of work and care he looked back at his life and hoped that he had been worthy to have been the owner of his pines.[26]

Native American, Chief Seattle, seems to be on the Journey of Works when he speaks of his people's stewardship:

> This we know: the earth does not belong to man, man belongs to the earth. All things are connected like the blood that unites us all. Man did not weave the web of life, he is merely a strand in it. Whatever he does to the web, he does to himself.[27]

Epictetus looked back on his life and wrote:

> What would you wish to be doing when you are found by death? I for my part would wish to be found doing something that belongs to a man, beneficent, suitable to the general interest. If death surprises me when I am busy about these things, it is good enough for me if I can stretch out my hands and say: the means which I have received for helping the world I have not neglected; I have not dishonored the world with my acts. That I have been given life, I am thankful. If I have used well the powers which are mine, I am content and give them back to the great life from which I came.[28]

IV. Journey of Harmony

The Journey of Harmony is the opposite polarity from the Journey of Works and carries the moon archetype, intuitive feeling (NF). Characteristics of the Journey of Harmony include: the quest for selfhood, mystical gratitude and expectancy, idealism, and a concentration on process in human relationships.

The first life focus for this Journey is to engage in a quest for authentic actualization, a quest for larger, deeper, selfhood. The great turning point in the ministry of Jesus came with his question to his disciples, "Who do you say that I am?" It is not only what you do, but who you are, that is essential. It is important that we work on ourselves, if we are going to influence the world, focus on being as well as doing. As it turned out his disciples, even his polar opposite, Peter, perceived his inner transformations.

In Emerson's essay, "Self-Reliance," we remember the lines:

> Life only avails, not the having lived. Power ceases in the instant of repose; it resides in the moment of transition from a past to a new state, in the shooting of the gulf, in the darting to an aim. This one fact the world hates; that the soul becomes; for that forever degrades the past, turns all riches to poverty, all reputation to a shame, confounds the saint with the rogue, shoves Jesus and Judas equally aside.[29]

Ralph Waldo Emerson, Unitarian minister and lecturer, American Transcendentalist and remarkable example of intuitive feeling, lunar spirituality (likely INFP).

The poet, Rainer Maria Rilke, said of this process of self knowing and growth:

> . . . out of this immersion in your own world, poems come, then you will not think of asking anyone whether they are good or not.[30]

The quest to understand the self fascinated biologist Loren Eiseley when he looked at future possibilities. There seems to be no limit to the extent of this exploration of the human self as a spiritual adventure. Eiseley says:

> Man is always partly of the future, and the future he possesses a power to shape. . . . Perhaps there may come to us . . . a ghostly sense that an invisible doorway has been opened—a doorway which widening out, will take man beyond the nature that he knows.[31]

This leads in to the mystic way of this journey, mystical harmony, gratitude, the attitude of expectancy, and healing dreams. This mystical experience is very different from the mystic clarity of the Journey of Unity. In the *Tao te Ching* we read:

> There is a thing confusedly formed.
> Born before heaven and earth.
> Silent and void
> It stands alone and does not change,
> Goes round and does not weary.
> It is capable of being the mother of the world.
> I know not its name
> So I style it 'the way.'
> I give it the makeshift name of 'the great.'
> Being great, it is further described as receding,
> Receding, it is described as far away,
> Being far away, it is described as turning back.[32]

In William Blake's words:

> To see a World in a Grain of Sand
> And a Heaven in a Wild Flower,
> Hold infinity in the palm of your hand
> And Eternity in an hour.[33]

One of the halls of worship, Baiyunguan, White Cloud Temple, the "philosophical" Taoist temple in Beijing, China, a gentle place in the midst of a booming city. Lao Tzu and Chuang Tzu, prominent sages, represent an intuitive feeling spirituality.

Chuang tzu said:

> Fishes are born in water
> Man is born in Tao. . . . .
> All the fish needs
> Is to get lost in Water.
> All man needs is to get lost
> In Tao.[34]

This vision of the Journey of Harmony can be powerfully persuasive in its non clarity and its non tangibility. It points to a hidden, vague, misty reality, far away and yet flowing near and all around and inside us. Rabindranath Tagore reports an early mystic experience that changed his life:

> When I was eighteen, a sudden spring breeze of religious experience
> for the first time came to my life and passed away leaving in my
> memory a direct message of spiritual reality. One day while I stood
> watching at early dawn the sun sending out its rays from behind the
> trees, I suddenly felt as if some ancient mist had in a moment lifted
> from my sight, and the morning light on the face of the world
> revealed an inner radiance of joy. The invisible screen of the
> common-place was removed from all things and all [persons] and
> their ultimate significance was intensified in my mind; . . . That
> which was memorable in this experience was its human message,
> the sudden expansion of my consciousness in the super-personal
> world of [humanity]. The poem I wrote on the first day of my
> surprise was named "The Awakening of the Waterfall". The
> waterfall, whose spirit lay dormant in its ice-bound isolation, was
> touched by the sun and, bursting in a cataract of freedom, it found
> its finality in an unending sacrifice, in a continual union with the
> sea. After four days the vision passed away, and the lid hung down
> upon my inner sight. In the dark, the world once again put on its
> disguise of the obscurity of an ordinary fact.[35]

One of my favorite ways to contrast this spirituality with others is in the story of Jesus and Nicodemus in the *Gospel of John*, a classic confrontation of the two Feeling spiritualities, NF with SF. Jesus launched into what to him was the evidence of spiritual reality. He said:

Brahmo Samaj Mandir or glass house for worship, erected by Debendranath Tagore in 1891, on the campus of his son, Rabindranath Tagore's ashram and school in Shantiniketan, West Bengal, India.

"You must be born anew. The wind blows where it wills, and you hear the sound of it, but you do not know whence it comes or whither it goes; so it is with everyone who is born of the Spirit." Nicodemus said to him, "How can this be?"[36]

But we remember it was Nicodemus later who wrapped the body of his leader after the crucifixion and lovingly placed him in the tomb.[37]

Those on the Journey of Harmony are possessed with social idealism. Jesus began his public ministry with a manifesto of ideas of what he would preach: the Beatitudes. Blessed are: "the poor in spirit," "those who mourn," "the meek," "those who hunger and thirst for righteousness," "the merciful," "the pure in heart," "the peacemakers." These would "inherit the earth."[38] His message was revolutionary but hard for many to see: doing good to those who hate you; loving your enemies; lending, expecting nothing in return. "It is easier for a camel to go through the eye of a needle than for a rich man to enter the kingdom of God."[39] People asked him when this Kingdom would come and he gave a typically perplexing answer:

> The kingdom of the Father is spread out on the earth, but people do not see it.[40]

The contemporary neo pagan leader, Starhawk, has the same kind of social idealism when she says:

> We are all longing to go home to some place we have never been— a place, half-remembered, and half-envisioned we can only catch glimpses of from time to time. Community. Somewhere, there are people to whom we can speak with passion without having the words catch in our throats. Somewhere a circle of hands will open to receive us, eyes will light up as we enter, voices will celebrate with us whenever we come into our own power. Community means strength that joins our strength to do the work that needs to be done. Arms to hold us when we falter. A circle of healing. A circle of friends. Someplace where we can be free.[41]

SCALE 1 INCH=1 FOOT.   COPYRIGHT·1905·BY·FREDERICK·WILSON·
·ARLINGTON· ST· CHURCH·
NORTH·SIDE

"Blessed are the Peacemakers" drawing, Tiffany Studios, memorial window to Alexander Strong Wheeler, Arlington Street Church, Boston, MA. The Beatitudes are a profound example of intuitive feeling spirituality.

There is a concern with process in this Journey, how we relate, not so much what we relate. Whitman wrote:

> I am larger, better than I thought, I did not know I held so much goodness.

> One's-self I sing, a simple separate person, Yet utter the word Democratic, the word En-Masse.[42]

What is the purpose of society, the purpose of congregations, if it is not to support individuals who will feel like this?!

Remember the incident of the feeding of the 5,000? They had only five loaves of bread and two sardines. But Jesus knew that even poor people don't leave home for a full day with no food. He divided the crowd into groups of fifty. They sat down on the hillsides, in these groups, face to face, and out came the food they had with them secreted away under their robes. They shared with each other. In the Journey of Harmony, process is an essential focus, bringing out that hidden, hopeful, mystic, humanity in people!

Many have found more than one of the Four Spiritualities so compelling as to make it difficult to choose their preferred journey from among them. We do, after all, have all four within us. In addition, we learned in childhood various spiritualities modeled in parents, family and community. We may have a model in mind from childhood experiences as to what ought to be the spiritual journey. Then in midlife and beyond we may have come into a greater balance with the differentiation of less preferred influences into consciousness. Not to resonate at all with one or more of the Four Spiritualities can indicate an overspecialization or interrupted growth towards wholeness. There are episodes in our lives when we are concentrating upon bringing an adjacent or opposing spirituality into a greater balance with our preferred spirituality, either because of our life-situation at the time or the ongoing call we all experience towards wholeness. It is therefore important to give all four ample reflection (see FIGURE 8). Of course your first hypothesis will be the journey which correlates with your type: the Journey of Unity, NT; the Journey of Devotion, SF; the Journey of Works, ST; and the Journey of Harmony, NF.

In the major branches of world religion, while the founder may be in one spirituality, the tradition broadened to include all four. A study of literature by and about a founder can yield a view of what their type may have been. That so many can see themselves reflected back from a beloved saint, prophet, teacher or sage, speaks of their profound development as persons and leaders but also of the rich interpretations from perspectives of all four spiritualities.

Journey	Journey of Unity ◯	Journey of Devotion ▢	Journey of Works ◉	Journey of Harmony ☽
cognitive orientation	principle truth	mantra direct personal experience	covenant, identity	actualization of self
mystical experience	clarity	devotional piety	work as practice	harmony, gratitude, healing dreams, expectancy
ethical concern	justice	service	stewardship	idealism, humane process

FIGURE 8 Characteristics of Four Spiritualities

The major religious cultures contain all four spiritualities practiced side by side. In the West we have Socrates for the Journey of Unity; Mohammed for its opposite, the Journey of Devotion; Moses in the Journey of Works; and Jesus in its opposite, the Journey of Harmony. These represent the founders of three great monotheistic religions and the tradition of Greek rationalism which has come down through the Enlightenment to the present.[43]

In India the four classic schools of yoga (Jnana, Bhakti, Karma and Raja) are directly parallel. Sankara or Rammohan Roy are in the Journey of Unity; Tulsidas or Ramakrishna are in its opposite, the Journey of Devotion; the great example of Arjuna in the *Bhagavad Gita* or Gandhi represent the Journey of Works; and Patanjali or Tagore are in its opposite, the Journey of Harmony.

In Chinese religion there was for centuries a dialectic between the Confucians (Confucius, Mencius and Hsun Tzu) for the Journey of Works, and their polar opposites, Lao Tzu and Chuang Tzu, for the Journey of Harmony. Then Buddhism entered China to give this religious culture greater balance. Like the Buddha, Bodhidharma, the founder of the Chan or Zen school, represents the Journey of Unity whereas many devotional practices combined with existing practices to meet the needs of the Journey of Devotion, for example the rich traditions which emerged around the worship of Kuan Yin.

Behind the great religious traditions we now experience are extremely ancient antecedents. What we know of the lives and teachings of some of the founders are mostly passed down to us in the oral tradition until literate scribes and scholars could fashion scriptures of the best and most treasured memories that came to them. But behind those we know and follow are a host of teachers who lived too long ago for their names and unique contributions to be known. Alphabets, languages, written literatures are a relatively recent development in human spiritual history. But we can find a narrative in the many clues to be found in myth and legend, architecture and religious artifacts. We now turn to this most ancient of stories.

The "Venus" of Willendorf, circa 20,000 B.C.,
Museum of Natural History, Vienna, Austria.

CHAPTER FOUR

OUR HUMAN EMERGENCE

In the beginning long long ago, over the course of the last four or five million years, what it is to be human, the stuff of our inner natures, began forming in a patient evolutionary process. We were born in the arms of mother earth. While many of us were devoured by tigers or drowned in floods, we were nurtured by the goddess earth. From her womb we were born, in her home and community we lived and to the warm darkness of her tomb we returned. We were closely attuned to her rhythms in the seasons when we gathered food and learned to collaborate with her cycles of abundance and her barren winters. We asked animals for their permission to be hunted for meat. Part of our nurture was an awareness that we kill to live. We felt our entire dependence with frequent rituals of gratitude and participation for it was critical to remain attuned. We lived completely within the garden of earth.

The earliest devotional objects we have found are small statues of female figures. Tiny hands and feet and featureless faces are attached to huge bodies with bulbous breasts and behinds so large in proportion that they resemble nurturing earth herself. The mother goddess projected no qualities of personhood, but rather of the matrix earth. She was pregnant with life. Her monthly fertility coordinated with the moon cycles as we see in the so-called Venus of Laussel with one hand holding the crescent moon (a bison horn) and the other placed on her abdomen. The sleeping goddess of Malta was found deep underground in a room carved for her in Paleolithic times. To grasp the power of the goddess one has only to imagine life in her realm. She was the queen bee and all activity and all meaning revolved around/within her presence.

The men hunted, building temples of initiation in deep caves. Even in this central male activity the perspective was of rebirth in the goddess. Boys at puberty were sent into the caves via long narrow tunnels barely wide enough to squeeze through, we might call rebirth canals. On completing this they came face to face with terrifying shamanic paintings of penetrating intensity. It was critical for them to separate from their mothers for men's work and to enter into the covenant of hunter with hunted. Coming face to face with a bison or bear is an awesome experience requiring preparation. And protecting the tribal territory from intruders was an equally sobering responsibility. Initiation caves are found on every continent. Lascaux is one of humanity's most profound temple centers.

There came a time in the Mesolithic age when climate changes gradually led to a scarcity of game. The women had been gathering grain so long that all could be fed without dependence upon the hunt. From the village women would find grain in a radius of several miles and bring it home. As they neared home the paths converged so that any grain that spilled by the side would germinate and grow nearer home, and after a few hundred years whole fields had developed making harvesting far easier. Men had the task of herding sheep and goats out on the hillsides and keeping animals out of the women's fields.

Never before or since has human leisure been in such plentiful supply. The men became quite bored after awhile. But women's Neolithic farming was so prosperous large surpluses developed and some of the men discovered the arts of trading and, later, banditry. Villages and grain silos were fortified. Men quickly lost much of their leisure. Defense and banditry fell to the strong. Trading was for the more intellectually inclined. You were on a steep learning curve if you wished to procure red ochre, or gold, or eventually a copper shield. We domesticated dromedaries and learned to build ships.

Nearly three-quarters of the planet is covered with water. It is not surprising that the oceans became the habitat for mariners. Aside from ledges and sand bars it is relatively easy to sail along the coast in sight of land. It is entirely different to sail out over the horizon into open expanses of sea as far as the eye can roam. If you have an idea of a destination you have to learn to navigate. The mariner's world is an abstract realm of trigonometry. Standing at the helm the captain triangulates through his mast the positions of sun, moon and stars. He has mapped the globe with invisible lines of longitude and latitude. Yes, he knows the earth is a sphere (though those back home will not believe such nonsense). And with the invention of a magnetic compass, identified in the Gilgemesh Epic as his "stones," he could plot his way across the seas. And he knows his way home to the family hearthside.

What does he find when he returns? Basically kinsfolk who live in a world between hills, five miles to the east, five miles to the west, a few miles upstream to more hills and downstream to the sea. Several of the men perhaps have walked to the next range of hills to negotiate with their neighbors. Like Ulysses in Tennyson's poem it would not take long before a certain restlessness set in, the call of adventure.

> I am part of all that I have met;
> Yet all experience is an arch where through
> Gleams that untraveled world whose margin fades
> Forever and forever when I move.

How dull it is to pause, to make an end,
To rust unburnished, not to shine in use![1]

Before the invention of the radio in the twentieth century, the captain of a ship had to comprehend the world he sailed and the ship he commanded as interfacing systems. He had to know logistics of food supply for his crew, timing for when to appear at his markets and what to sell to them, he had to have some idea of meteorological conditions of the seasons, navigation of course, the anthropology of peoples along the way (whether they were peaceful or cannibals) when he put in to replenish their water supply, he needed some idea of motivational psychology, had to be tough minded on issues of discipline and strategic decision making and negotiating in his trading relations, he had to be a master of ship repair. In short he required a broad and comprehensive understanding of how the world works, its integrating principles. He was a man steeped in possibilities for unlocking new avenues of trade, open to new ideas, willing to adventure. He was a problem solver.

His world was quite different than the profoundly traditional society of his wife and mother back home. For them the goddess was always present. At every hand her fecundity was displayed. The seas gave rise to the male divinity, a god who was not present, but absent, an abstract reality out there in the firmament, sky. It was a world of imagination, not of tangibles. In the abstract world of trigonometry and possibilities the consequences of poor judgment were no less absolute. On land for violating the integrity of the domain of the goddess you could be banished or given punishments of hard labor. On the sea you could sink to the bottom and never be heard from again.

The spirituality of the mariners, under the omni-awesome sky, was the abstract worship of an absent god An occasional *Psalm* captures its essence:

When I look at thy heavens, the work of thy fingers,
the moon and the stars which thou hast established;
what is man that thou art mindful of him,
and the son of man that thou dost care for him?
Yet thou hast made him little less than God,
and dost crown him with glory and honor.
Thou hast given him dominion over the works of thy hands;
. . . the birds of the air, the fish of the sea,
whatever passes along the paths of the sea.[2]

This is the world of the adventurer, the world of an abstract god, the global vision of mariners along "the paths of the sea." It is not the nurturing world of intimate village life, amidst the planting and harvesting of fields of grain.

One of the great heroes of this new sky world of adventure was Hercules and his twelve labors. When he fought the Lernaean Hydra, a dragon with nine heads mired in quicksand and mud, he would slice off a head with his sword and another would grow. He would begin to win the battle and slam the hydra down onto the ground and she would spring up revitalized and full of fury. It was only when he placed his battle into a wider perspective, that he realized that earth sustained the hydra, that he could only win by lifting the dragon into the light, the atmosphere, and strength drained from the dragon and she expired. This is a classic story of men coming into a separate consciousness, of the opening of sky as the polar opposite energy of earth. The unity of the world was now two, the male and the female god and goddess, the primary polarity of life.

Hercules and the Lernaean Hydra or a differentiating of sky from earth.
National Museum of Athens, Greece.

We have described one third of the Archetype of the Spirit in our story thus far, the primary polarity of earth and sky. Since psychological type according to Jung is the way consciousness differentiates in our human nature we would naturally expect it to be at the center of this polarity. The combination of the sensing (S) and feeling (F) functions (SF) characterizes an earth spirituality. We may enter directly and tangibly into religious experience. The objects of devotion are not distant but immediately at hand in the food, water, shelter, trees, fields and relationships of life. Here is birth and death, physical and spiritual. Here and now the community surrounds us in nurture and support. The goddess sleeps in winter, awakens in spring in her youth, gives birth and matures in summer and fall, later to rest again. Hers are the great seasonal festivals of fertility and planting, harvesting and gratitude. She is life bursting from the soil of her being. She is the spring of the woodland deer and the power of the prairie bison. She can bless a newborn infant and she can wear a necklace of skulls (Kali) and dance on the body of a fallen god (Shiva). Earth spirituality combines sensing (S), a direct employing of the five senses, sensing inward parts, focusing upon present actualities and memories of similar realities past, with feeling (F), the rational cognition of emotional content into evaluations of value, our grasp of humane and appropriate responses in all levels of our relationships, parenting, marriage, friendship, citizenship, leadership. Sensing (S) is the most extensive function, embodied, connecting us back with all living beings. Its primordial development gives it incredible sophistication, and being a non verbal experiencing in the present most of what it "knows" it does not speak of. Matched with feeling (F) it expresses itself in direct relational qualities giving earth spirituality a substantial quiet pervasive power that is felt through a receptive entering into its presence. Earth traditions are our oldest religious observances, eliciting intense loyalties which remain at the foundations of all other spiritual enterprises.

Opposite earth is sky, the archetypal orientation for those who combine intuition (N) with thinking (T). Intuition always embraces the larger more inclusive and expansive perspective, looking for possibilities in a thing, person or situation. Rather than tangible and local (S) intuition (N) scans for the global and abstract. Behind what is seen or heard are the patterns, systems from which all which we see and hear emanate. Intuition (N) finds them and thinking (T) names, analyzes and categorizes them as operant principles. Intuition matched with thinking seeks to understand the big picture, to integrate the world with an embracing truth. And as the adventurer, pioneer, researcher, strategist, they will continue the search for ever larger integrations. This search can range far from the everyday, out into systems cohering universe, the god-like energies. Imagine Polynesian mariners, Akkadian ship captains, or magi in lonely towers, looking out at the motions of the heavens, studying as in historic times Copernicus, or Galileo, or Newton, or Einstein studied.

Where sky and earth meet, the world of the mariners. Seen off Quoddy Head, Lubec, ME.

Faith always begins with doubts and questions, it must be discovered anew, congruent with all else, intentional, open. When the larger vision is captured, when the thoroughgoing investigation is carried forward, when beauty, truth, goodness are comprehended, then sky religion reveals its findings to the world. Alas, the world often does not welcome such radical input. Others may only resonate with bits and pieces shattering the profound unity that has been discovered. Thus the intuitive thinking (NT) initiatives may retreat to the periphery of religious communities, or form elites of intellectual power, or indeed set off upon new adventures of discovery.

Such is the life of sky religion. The earliest adventurers who journeyed far, if not over deserts and seas then in the searching mind, broke apart the primeval oneness. One became two, earth and sky in polar opposition. This polarity energized the human emergence on the planet. History became possible. Sensing feeling (SF) spirituality symbolized by the square was opposed and complemented by intuitive thinking (NT) spirituality symbolized by the single circle in the primary polarity of our Archetype of the Spirit (FIGURE 9).

FIGURE 9 Primary Polarity

Indeed perspectives of earth and sky were so far apart, mediating influences were required if human society was to harness this vast liberation of opposing energies for its wellbeing. To return to our story, the mariners would return home from their long voyages from time to time and they would reveal their primary orientation to the sky god. But this sky god was rather remote, profound but absent. Earth peoples were

Carl Jung's Bollingen Stone, showing the secondary polarity of sun and moon.
Figure in the center is Asklepios according to Jung's autobiography,
Memories, Dreams, Reflections. Bollingen, Switzerland.

somewhat skeptical that he actually existed! The Psalmists also knew this feeling of rejection by family, friends, kinsfolk:

> My God, my God, why hast thou forsaken me?
> Why art thou so far from helping me,
> from the words of my groaning?
> O my God, I cry by day, but thou dost not answer;
> and by night, but find no rest.[3]

It was in situations such as this that the mariner would turn to his kinsfolk and point to the sun. You can see the sun, you can feel its warmth, surely he is dependable. The cosmos is indeed vast with profound distances of space and time. Nature it is said abhors a vacuum and thus on the right hand of sky sun comes in. If sky is to the north on our compass, sun is in the west. Sun revolves in a great arc bringing light into the day, powerful at noontime and brilliant in its "setting" when earth eclipses its presence and radiations of color through the atmosphere herald the promise of his return. For the mariner the sun drops into the sea and there are stories of heroes and kings at death, placing their souls upon ships to sail west after the sun into the next life.

Most basically sun is visible as if sky intended to be represented in a life giving and definitive way, bringing the comprehensive vision to earth in unmistakable revelations of light. Since time immemorial this has been the role of sun's revolutions revealed to humans in fatherly form or in the form of the great winged solar disk. In tribal lore of the American Indian the sun makes his rounds each day to insure the world order is maintained. In many places the sun became central when city states came into being. There came a time when society became so complex the direct and relatively "democratic" or consensual rule of tribal elders and wise women became ineffective. The Neolithic agricultural surplus nurtured increasingly large populations concentrated in cities, specialists in writing, architecture, religion, medicine, production of pottery, clothing, carpentry, brick making, blacksmithing, transportation and warfare emerged. Trading activities accumulated wealth, introducing ideas and customs unsettling for the social order.

When chaos erupted warriors took control to reestablish order. Kings were set upon thrones and looked around for advisors to help them establish order and cohesion once again. This is when what R. Buckminster Fuller called "the navigator priests" were called in from the world of the mariners.[4] The kings were strong men. What did they know of the larger picture? The elite advisors give them their first principle: be sure no one knows everything we will reveal to you, particularly the warriors. Thus hierarchies of specialists were established. The kings built large ziggurats and towering temples and at appointed times climbed them to converse with the winged solar disk. Hammurabi came down from his ziggurat with a code of laws for the moral and social administration of the empire.[5] Picture Moses descending the mountain his face shining like the sun! Moses, the lawgiver, was an archetypal sun figure.[6] It was about this time that the Western Semites invented the alphabet with its explosive impact for authority in complex social orders and soon, written scriptures. Apollo to the north was a more unruly sun god, rising in the east at Delos, coming to full zenith at Delphi, setting at Epidaurus.[7] This was the age of the Pandavas, of Krishna and Rama in India. The Shang dynasty was turning out bronze ritual vessels in China with the enlightened reigns of Yao and Shun.

There were wise kings like Solomon or Akbar and there were rather ugly ones like

Winged solar disk, Shamash, instructing and ordaining King Ashurnasirpal at the tree of life, Assyrian, Nimrod Palace, circa 865 BC, British Museum, London, England.

Detail of winged solar disk

Herod or King Hsüan of Ch'i, who lost the "Mandate of Heaven."[8] The solar rulers at their best brought sky to earth and stewarded the well being of their peoples. But when the standards were compromised the world could be rather cruel, devoid of sympathy or compassion, even with the vision of an Akhenaton or a Marcus Aurelius.

In such times the saviors would arise. We first see them riding the crescent moon, infants in the arms of the beautiful virgin goddess, in sculpture and painting, Isis holding Horus, riding the moon, or young Mary holding the infant Jesus. The moon reflects a gentle light, reminding us of earthly values, that mysterious connection we have with all life, with each other, a longing and relational affirmation.[9] The goddess is holding her gift for humanity, her son, who will enter the world as a living sacrifice for all we long for, not only the order of sun but the love borne of the lunar night. Emerson called these the poet-prophets[10]; Isaiah, the servant "man of sorrows."[11] They come as avatars, saviors and often martyrs.

The rise of the waxing moon each evening has always fascinated mystics and the sentimental, watching the large orange globe rise until at its zenith it is smaller and white, and admiring its trail over the waters. There have long been new moon and full moon celebrations. Early calendars were all tied to the lunar cycles. Imagine whole villages where the women's menstrual cycles followed the moon's so as to cohere all rhythms of tribal life in a single pattern. We have long lost that biological coherence. In a world of street lights, highway traffic and security lighting, most of us today have no idea whether the moon is waxing or waning, crescent or full. Still however, more babies are born at the full moon and in Islamic and a few other societies the lunar calendar prevails.

There is a close relationship between the moon as a symbol and the serpent for as the snake sheds its skin and grows another the moon sheds its light and comes back to its fullness. The moon is tied closely to planting and harvesting cycles. Likewise the bull, whose horns resemble the crescent moon, is sacrificed and his blood is sprinkled over the newly sown fields. In some societies such as ancient Crete it was the young king who was sacrificed from his moon throne. Death and resurrection were central themes of lunar traditions and thus of the great saviors in historic times: Osiris, Dionysos, Christ.

Moon energies rise from the earth even as the moon revolves around the planet. The moon goddesses, however, hardly resemble the mother goddess. They appear in "drop dead" beauty and cannot be ignored by even the sturdiest solar warrior.[12] As the solar divinities come towards earth from sky with messages of social reform and order, the lunar goddess and her sons rise from earth towards sky with messages of mercy and harmony. "What does it profit you if you gain the whole world and lose your soul?" In historic time a prevailing pattern is that every action sparks a reaction. As Carl Jung pointed out, our dreams often point to that in our lives which most needs to be

Akhenaton and family enjoying solar blessings.
Egyptian Museum, Cairo, Egypt.

brought back into balance. When solar order rules the day, the lunar night brings us back to ourselves in wholeness, that is if we heed the messages revealed. As earth nurture brought into being sky adventure, so also sun social order has brought into being moon relational harmony.

> The heavens are lasting and the earth enduring.
> The reason the world is able to be lasting and enduring
> Is because it does not live for itself.
> Thus it is able to be long-lived.
>
> It is on this model that the sages withdraw their persons from
>   contention yet find themselves out in front.
> Put their own persons out of mind yet find themselves taken care of.
> Isn't it simply because they are unselfish that they can satisfy
>   their own needs?[13]

Solar image of the Czech Unitaria logo.
Prague, Czech Republic.

Those conversant with psychological type will recognize the solar aspect of the archetype as sensing and thinking (ST) and its opposite, the moon aspect of the archetype, as intuitive and feeling (NF). Together they form the secondary polarity of the Archetype of the Spirit. Solar spirituality shares its rational function, thinking (T), with sky but being tangibly oriented (S) rather than globally oriented (N) it brings sky insights towards earth into practical, grounded realistic applications. Lunar spirituality shares its rational function, feeling (F), with earth but being globally oriented (N) rather than tangibly oriented (S) it brings earth connections towards sky into idealistic and humane applications. This secondary polarity of sun (ST) and moon (NF) come into their own and reach their greatest strength about midway between earth and sky thus forming centers at the west and east cardinal points of the circle (FIGURE 10).

This completes two thirds of the Archetype of the Spirit (the circular compass aspects) and provides a good place to pause for two critical considerations. First, our story thus far has been largely in historical time. It is really the actualization of the archetype in the collective consciousness in the dimension of historic time. But the archetype has resided in the human unconscious from primeval origins. It is the nature of archetypes that they are there, and their presence is usually but dimly apprehended by the conscious side of us. A Navaho shaman, or Mesopotamian priest, or Taoist sage may draw renditions of the archetype motifs in local genres. But they are all drawing on the same archetype. While the emergence of the archetype in its four aspects has appeared at different points in time, generally in a pattern of earth, then sky, then in quick succession sun and moon, the archetype itself has always been active in the shadows of the unconscious.

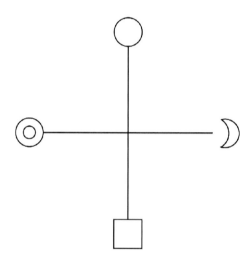

FIGURE 10 Primary and Secondary Polarities

A leader in the theory of psychological type, the late James Newman, in his studies of cognitive psychology, created a model of type and brain interface.[14] In understanding his model it is essential to remember that the two hemispheres operate independently, circulating from the cerebral cortices down through "lower" levels and back. In his view extraversion (E) and introversion (I), for example, would operate through the thalamus and reticular reflex system, associating from the thalamus independently in the two hemispheres. On each of the cerebral cortices he places the judging function in the frontal and the perceiving function in the posterior. The judging functions regulate the perceiving functions. Contrary to the volume of "right brain–left brain" popular literature he finds overwhelming evidence for thinking (T) and intuition (N) on the left and feeling (F) and sensing (S) on the right. The left hemisphere he identifies as the "intellectual sphere" and the right as the "experiential sphere." The left judging function (T) cognizes input from perception in terms of naming, logic, analysis, arranging patterns into systems. Input from intuition (N) is stronger and more direct than from sensing (S), thus the powerful global orientation of intuitive thinking (NT). It is far more verbal as the right hemisphere may gain as much as a middle school vocabulary and grammar. At the right or experiential sphere we see the cognition of emotional experience in what he calls a "symphony of

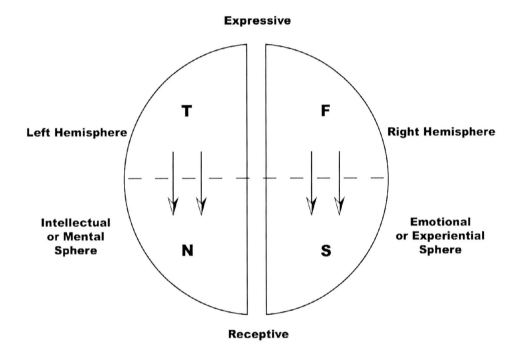

FIGURE 11 Newman's Model of Type/Hemisphere Correspondences

appropriateness," judging in constructs of social norms and values. This valuation has a stronger more direct input from sensing (S) than from intuition (N) hence the deep and direct grounding of sensing feeling (SF) (see FIGURE 11).

James Newman is careful to warn that "a model is not the territory." The value of a model is that it simplifies, providing a shorthand for understanding the bold significances of complex systems. With perhaps 100 billion nerve cells in the living brain, having evolved to its present form over tens of millions of years building

*Cow with lunar horns, perhaps Hathor, Queen Hatshepant's Temple,
Valley of the Queens, Luxor, Egypt.*

*Lunar symbol of Islam on the dome of Bayt al-Mal, Mosque of Amr Ibn Al-as,
oldest in a city of 1,000 minarets, Cairo, Egypt.*

complexity upon complexity, a model only opens the door to further exploration. He also stressed that research on the human brain has helped us flesh out and adapt our understandings of type, particularly of the feeling function (F) and sensing feeling (SF). The work of Antonio Damasio, for example, reminds us that all mental activity derives from the mapping of body states. This is done in a kind of emotional wash, the primary way we regulate our bodies and thereby our perceptions and relationships in all that surrounds us. Feelings are the monitoring of our emotional states, "the feeling of what happens." Responding upon these structures of feeling, arise consciousness and an autobiographical self. Damasio's work supports Newman to the extent that he finds a hemispheric specialization, language on the left side, emotional processing on the right. I would speculate that the work of Damasio, Churchland, Lakoff, Johnson and others will bring sensing feeling in as a baseline at the center of all else in type, with the intuiting and thinking functions conceptualized as more specialized and dependent.[15] This is how I have now described their emergence historically as well.

It can be readily seen how Newman's model correlates powerfully with the primary polarity in the Archetype of earth (SF) and sky (NT). The secondary polarity of sun (ST) and moon (NF) mediate/balance the world between the hemispheres. Critically in both Newman's model and in the Archetype, communication between the hemispheres is weaker than within the hemispheres as it must flow back and forth in the corpus callosum. Thus the left judging function (T) is weaker in regulating sensing for sensing thinking (ST) than in regulating intuition for intuitive thinking (NT). Likewise the right judging function (F) is weaker in regulating intuition for intuitive feeling (NF) than sensing for sensing feeling (SF). We find therefore in sun orientations a less regulated more free wheeling sensing perceiving (dominant introverted sensing as in ISTJ and dominant extraverted sensing as in ESTP). In moon orientations we find a less regulated more free wheeling intuitive perceiving (dominant introverted intuition as in INFJ and dominant extraverted intuition as in ENFP). Conversely for intuitive feeling types (NF), feeling judging has some direct connection with sensing (S) and for intuitive thinking types (NT), least direct connection with sensing (S). For sensing thinking types (ST) thinking judging has some direct connection with intuition (N) and sensing feeling types (SF) have least direct connection with intuition (N). For understanding the complementary nature of types this model increases our awareness of the uniqueness of each of the sixteen types. We all have all four functions within us (S, N, T, F) but in differing measure. And we all have all four combinations within us, earth (SF), sky (NT), sun (ST), and moon (NF) and the differences between the primary and secondary polarities and within them (particularly in the secondary/mediating polarity) adds great richness as we explore pathways to spiritual wholeness.

Albrecht Dürer, "Fire Rains from Heaven," engraving, shows the earth - sky (heaven) and sun - moon polarities, with an apparent sky bias. (reprinted in E. Edinger, Ego and Archetype, Dover Publications)

Albrecht Dürer, "The Great Crucifixion," engraving, has the earth - sky, sun - moon motif
but with an extreme sky bias, showing the the secondary polarity at the seventh rather than
the fourth chakra. The cross of course is the tree of life as well. (reprinted
in Joseph Campbell, The Inner Reaches of Outer Space, *Harper & Row)*

Ceiling design for the Battistero degli Ariani, Arian Baptistry, Ravenna, Italy.
The archetype of earth—sky, and perhaps sun—moon as well are intact with a Moses
type figure on the left and John the Baptist on the right.

*Buddhist stele beside a path on Mt. Hiei near Kyoto, Japan.
Earth to sky motif can be 'read' here with the Buddha
accompanied by solar and lunar companions.*

Bodhi Tree (an offshoot of the original) where the Buddha achieved enlightenment,
Bodh Gaya, Bihar Province, India.

CHAPTER FIVE

THE WORLD TREE

The motif of the tree, the sacred tree of life, is found in all branches of human culture. It has two elements of about equal size. Its roots spread deep and wide in the dark earth receiving nurture there and storing its life's work of replenishment. Its trunk, branches, leaves above ground all reach through its crown towards sky, for atmosphere (CO_2) and light. Within sky of course comes the life giving energy of sun. Branches and leaves bend towards the sun. In recent times we have learned of our symbiotic relationship with the tree. As we breathe in oxygen and breathe out carbon dioxide the tree absorbs carbon dioxide and releases oxygen into the atmosphere. It is literally as well as symbolically the tree of life.

But as a symbol we revere the tree. It lives in two realms, one exposed to the light of day, the other rooted in shadow and hidden from our sight, analogous to our consciousness and our unconscious, the known and the equally active unknown. The tree we see is subject to the winds of weather, bending in moving currents. Things spiritual are always associated with air, breathing, light (or enlightenment), the atmosphere of life. But the tree is also rooted firm, remaining in place at the source of its nurture, must remain connected to one landscape, immobile. Things having to do with soul, deepening, enriching our lives are always associated with our commitments, rooted in human relationships. The tree symbolizes the interaction of spirit and soul. While we know our human nature requires locomotion, action, adaptability, change, we also appreciate the need for our responsible connection with relatives, neighbors, all levels of interaction in human society for we are social animals.

The human spine, with its nervous system branching out in all directions from it is a kind of internal analogy to the tree. At the base of the spine are the primal energies of earth, our sexual natures, the vitality of abdomen, our physical powers and attachments. Along the spine, midway is the heart where the primary and secondary polarities cross, or where energies coming in from the compass points are made whole, then radiating outward from the center in rhythmic pulse. The heart is the center, the axis mundi of the Archetype of the Spirit. Continuing towards the crown of the head are the more intangible intellectual balances of life. Here are centers for

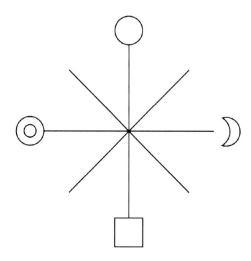

FIGURE 12 Archtype of the Spirit and human body

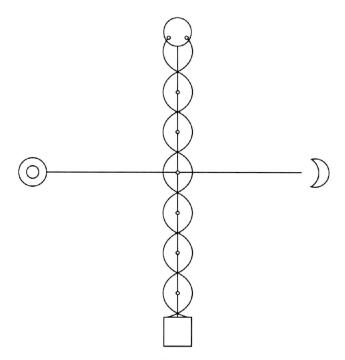

FIGURE 13A Archtype of the Spirit with caduceus

rational and mystical oneness, the largest embraces and affirmations of life. Equally, stretching towards the base, is the energetic reintegration of the vital body to monitor and prepare the way for bodily wellbeing, the emotional states and foundation for all else. Here too we see the contrasts of soul enriching experiences from the heart towards the base and from the heart towards the crown, a stretching for spiritual enlightenment.[1]

If you were to stand with arms and legs extending 45 degrees from the spine you would form a large X crossing at the heart (FIGURE 12). Between the outstretching arms is the sphere of sky, between the right arm and right leg is the sphere of sun, between the two legs is the sphere of earth, and between the left leg and left arm is the sphere of the rising moon. How remarkable that at the center of this body and forward of the spine at its midpoint is the beating heart flanked on either side by the breathing lungs. We live each day within the model of our individual and collective Archetype of the Spirit. It can thus be perceived both externally and internally, shared by all kinsfolk in the human family.

One of the clearest examples of our archetype can be found in the traditions of India. The spine is represented as containing seven centers or chakras for spiritual

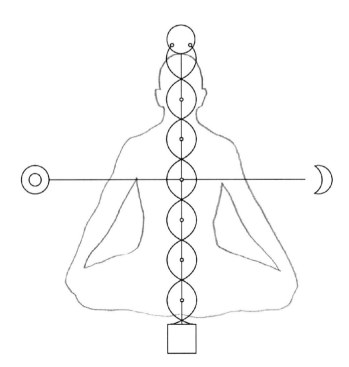

FIGURE 13B Archtype superimposed on yogin

awareness. The goal of the system is to integrate all through a process of awakening each one in succession. The fourth center is the heart chakra, with three below relating to the body, sexuality and vitality; and with three above relating to communication, the world of the gods/goddesses, and enlightenment itself. Each chakra must be awakened and attuned to the vibrations of all before moving on to the next. This process is known as the rising of sushuma, a serpent, for the spine taken literally in its bone, sheath and flexibility has a serpent-like quality.[2]

There are two other serpents which together assist the awakening of the chakras, weaving their way around the spine so as to reveal the seven centers. On the left is Ida or the lunar serpent and on the right is Pingala or the solar serpent. This is found universally as the caduceus which is an elaboration of the Archetype of the Spirit. It is associated with the healing arts as would be expected when the whole archetype is brought into coordination and balance, the goal of spiritual wholeness (FIGURE 13). The staff of the caduceus with the interweaving serpents is often shown with a bird above the serpents' heads, a symbol of sky or enlightenment. A number of older bishop's staffs when not shepherds crooks were the caduceus. In Central America one sees interwoven serpents' bodies each with the head of a bird, as with Quetzalcoatl.[3] In the Sumarian city of Lagash on the libation cup of King Gudea there are two interweaving serpents forming seven chakras.[4] They are the inner sanctum of a shrine guarded by two winged leopards implying a sky orientation. In Crete it is the goddess who holds the two serpents in her right and left hands, her feet on the ground, the bird of sky/enlightenment on her head.

In the archetype sun is always on the right hand of sky and moon is always on the left hand of sky. Looking at it from an earth perspective, the opposite is the case. Moon always rises to the right of earth and sun descends towards earth to the left. Being dwellers of the earth we usually visualize it in this way. When in diagram, picture or iconic form we perceive it from an earth stance (FIGURE 13). However, for example, when we read in *Ephesians*[5] that after the resurrection Christ sat at the right hand of God, he was placed in the solar position.[6] When we first introduced the Christ figure he was riding the crescent moon in his mother's lap. Most heroes and saviors who came into the world as "suffering servants," and die and are resurrected are lunar figures, as was Osiris for example before him. However, with the spread of Christianity in the second and third centuries and with its eventual acceptance as the state religion of the Roman Empire the Christ figure was preempted and given a golden halo, symbol of solar figures. When not preempted in numinous attraction with the polar opposition of sun and moon, they go into battle. A persistent motif in Persian and Assyrian imagery, for example, is the pouncing of the solar lion onto the back of the lunar bull, consuming it and all its lunar energies.[7] The solar hero, Mithras, is seen riding a bull and plunging his sword through the bull's heart.

Above: *Naga steles under tree at Sri Ranga Patnam fort in South India. Note seven headed serpent on lunar side.*

Naga (serpent) steles beside tree, Sri Rranga Patnum Fort, South India. Serpents, like vines, often entwine or are at trees, being the creative motion in the tree of life.

*Naga (serpent) worship at an ant hill inhabited by cobras,
Sri Ranga Patnam Fort, South India.*

Imperial dragons, southern stairways to Qi Nian Dian
at the Tian Tan, Temple of Heaven, Beijing, China.
Note the solar dragon moving toward earth
and the lunar dragon ascending toward sky.

Menhir aux serpents, a Paleolithic stone monument among dozens in the Celtic "alignements de Kermario" near Carnac, France.

Altar of the Caduceus, Aztec, 15th century. Reprinted
in several works by Joseph Campbell.

*Libation Cup of King Gudea of Lagash, Sumer. Six chakras lead to a
seventh, the contents of the cup itself! Winged leopards occupy the
solar and lunar positions. The swords are interesting perhaps
indicating the preemption of martial passions by spiritual ritual practices.*

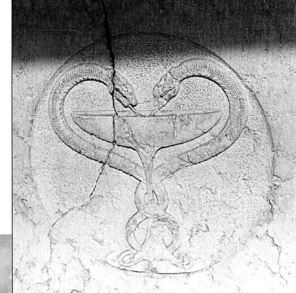

Serpents and wine cup, Venice, Italy.

Detail of iron fence, Yale University, New Haven, CT. A flame (of knowledge?) replaces the dove or bird of enlightenment. The caduceus archetype rises from the unconscious in numerous contexts, for example in Matthew 10, "be wise as serpents and innocent as doves."

Seven-headed serpent, Channekeshava Temple at Belur, South India.
A majority of the heads are hidden in the deep shadows of this ancient temple.

Snake Goddess from Knossos,
Museum of Herakleion, Crete.

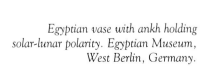

Egyptian vase with ankh holding
solar-lunar polarity. Egyptian Museum,
West Berlin, Germany.

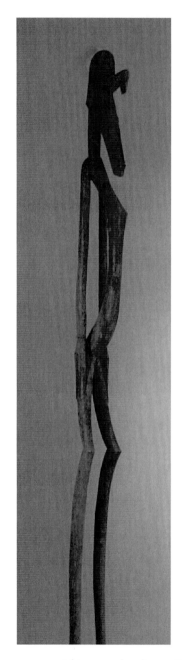

African wood sculpture. Female figure with bird of enlightment
atop her head. Author's collection.

A typical theme of religious art of Mithraism where the solar savior (Mithras) plunges a sword into the lunar bull. It replicates an ancient Persian motif where a lion is seen sinking its claws and teeth into the back of a bull. (from, Maarten Vermaseren's Corpus Inscriptionum et Monumentorum Religionis Mithriacae, and republished by Oxford University Press.)

Window in Chapel of St. Ludmilla, St. Vitus's Cathedral, Prague,
Czech Republic (designed by Max Svobinsky in 1934), has the
archetype form with focus upon the holy spirit (dove) and its
radiations of light.

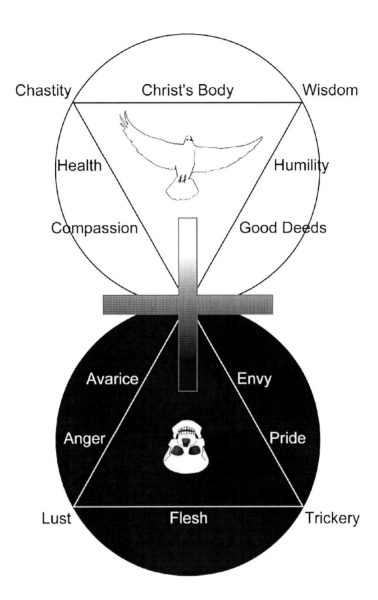

FIGURE 14 Boehme's Mandala

Mithraism was a major rival religion in the Roman Empire especially popular in the Roman legions. Thus in the disciplines of achieving wholeness through awakening the seven chakras it is important to understand what both your left hand and your right hand are doing as you seek to balance the spiritual energies along the way.

The Christian mystic, Jacob Boehme, created a rather striking mandala image (FIGURE 14), "Die Wiedergebuhrt" or the "The Rebirth."[8] It consists of two spheres, an upper sphere of rebirth and a lower sphere of first birth which touch at the heart chakra on a cross. The lower sphere is dark, like the roots of a tree in the earth, with seven centers or crosses to bear on an equilateral triangle including pride, anger, lust, avarice, envy, trickery, sins of the flesh. At the center of the dark sphere is a skull at the base of the cross. In the upper light sphere are seven centers on an equilateral triangle, each with a human eye, representing good deeds, humility, compassion, health, chastity, wisdom, representing for Boehme "Christ's body." At the crown of the cross in the center of the sphere is a bird upon a heart with the inscription *John 3:5*. Other Biblical references are to *Psalm 51* a call to repentance and to *Zechariah* indicating that the seven eyes are "eyes of the Lord which range through the whole earth." (4:10) Like the seven chakras of the yoga traditions one has the impression that each was opened through a spiritual transformation. But it appears this process only occurred as one of the seven in the lower sphere was closed, a cessation of the gross body and an opening of the spiritual "body of Christ," an eternal state free of time and space as represented by the skull in the lower sphere, a reminder of our mortality. Whereas in the yoga traditions the equilateral triangles of earth and sky are superimposed at the heart chakra forming a six-pointed star of transformation, in Boehme's mandala they meet but do not mesh.[9] The earth body is repressed, not transformed, and one is absorbed in sky. While this process seems to have worked for

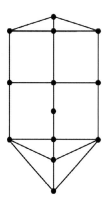

FIGURE 15 Sifirot

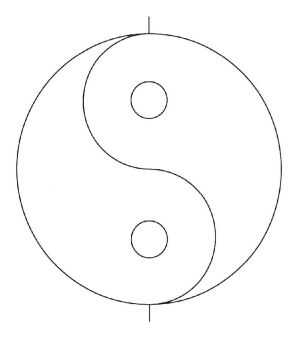

FIGURE 16 Yin Yang

the individual mystic, Boehme, for the collective this extreme rejection of earth leaves enduring tensions of unresolved energies.

The Jewish Kabbalah image of the tree of life or Sifirot (FIGURE 15) is an important ancient cousin of Boehme's model.[10] Tradition places it as a creation of God so that it could be seen as a reflection for God's own self perception. Thus it is posited as a perfect model of the God-human interaction even as its lowest levels are biological, its mid-ranges psychic and its upper ranges closer to the Divine will. It can be seen as an instrument for spiritual disciplines gradually balancing our natures across these thresholds of transformation. The central spine of the Sefirot has seven chakras, three of them polarities with female and male valences, not unlike the lunar and solar serpents with these valences respectively in yogic traditions. The Sifirot is an important variation because while as in Boehme's mandala there is a "higher" and "lower" distinction the energies do flow in both directions.

The Yin-Yang symbol of China (FIGURE 16) is wholly neutral in the up-down dimension. It is a model of eternal circulation, with lunar energies circulating one way and solar energies circulating the other, the lunar containing an "eye" of earth, the solar containing an "eye" of sky. To compare it with the other holistic models one must imagine a vertical spine behind this circulation. It is a humanistic-naturalistic mandala.

FIGURE 17

Axial great corn plant

A Navaho sand painting tradition is described by Joseph Campbell, the pollen path through the "axial great corn plant," a version of the tree of life (FIGURE 17).[11] There is a large corn plant forming the spine of the mandala. It has three roots at the base guarded by the Spirit Bringers. The image at first glance looks like the staff of Asklepios with one serpent entwining the spine rather than two. Here however the coiled structure is a rainbow extending as far as the heart chakra, there suddenly changing to a lightening bolt to the top of the stalk whereon is perched a bird of enlightenment. The rainbow has two colors, red representing solar energy and blue representing water and the moon. Two figures are placed in the secondary polarity on either side of the heart chakra, both sons of the sky/sun god, Tsóhanoai, who also produced the lightening bolt. The pollen path is a collective tribal process, the culmination of which, at the lightening bolt, ecstatically transports the participant towards enlightenment. There is considerable integration of earth and sky here, as the two sons in coming back from their father into the tribal domain of earth experienced a passage, assisted by the talking god, Hastyéyali, recharging their energy appropriately for community living. It is Hastyéyali who possesses both lunar and solar powers of the rainbow.

I owned a painting of the Christmas manger scene for years before, looking at it anew, I realized its deeper power is in the archetype informing the painting (FIGURE 18). The infant in straw is placed upon mother earth, the angels above are emissaries of father sky. They are even carrying words: "Gloria In Excelsis Deo." On the left as we face it, is an old man with a white beard, looking more like Moses than young Joseph, holding a staff reminding us of the time when Moses threw down his staff before Pharaoh and it transformed into a serpent. And then Mary, on the right as we face it, is very young and concave as the crescent moon, pondering all that we know in her heart. To emphasize the lunar significance of the Christ child in this nighttime birth there is a horned cow in the background. It is a beautiful family scene, but with the whole power of our Archetype of the Spirit, that power that we all know deep within us.

In these and many other examples, we see spiritual awakening, development, and "progress" energized in the primary polarity of earth and sky. In most mandalas of the archetype there is a model of progression from earth towards sky, from the gross body to the sublime body, from darkness to light. On the face of it this presents a problem for understanding this system as the archetype behind the Four Spiritualities. I endorse the rule in typology that all sixteen types are of equal worth and society is only truly whole when it honors the gifts of all and understands how this diversity is mutually complementary.[12] If we begin with the premise that from the beginning human spirituality has been of, by and for all types in the Four Spiritualities Mandala then we may see that the vision of wholeness has been corrupted in some local traditions. There has been a bias towards sky and away from earth.[13] Restoring the

Manger scene as an example of the Archetype of the Spirit. The infant rests in a manger grounded in earth, while angels with their banner, "Gloria In Excelsus Deo," represent sky. Figure on left with white hair and beard holding a staff is reminiscent of the solar Moses whereas Mary's posture is unmistakenly lunar in form, reinforced by the horns of the cow beside her. The archetype form adds great power (largely unconscious) to the nativity scene, from the author's collection.

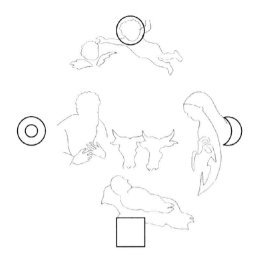

FIGURE 18 Manger scene

dynamic balance of our Archetype of the Spirit must be a priority for both collective and individual well-being.

We have discussed how as the primary polarity moved from the collective unconscious into the collective consciousness (and thence for some into the dynamics of individual consciousness as well) the sky orientation seemed remote and absent while the earth orientation seemed so omnipresent that after sky was differentiated earth seemed confining, even smothering. Sky adventure became too remote and earth nurture became too present. Hence the secondary polarity came into conscious attention. Sun circled from sky towards earth. In response, moon circled from earth towards sky. Along the spine of the archetype as we move closer towards sky we begin to shed the "baggage" of our lives. This is what the word enlighten in large part means. We lighten the load. In order to travel closer to the light we practice subtractive spiritual disciplines. The yogin often has no more possessions than his loincloth. The highest order of Jain monks are "sky clad." When the rich young man asked Jesus "What shall I do to inherit eternal life? Jesus replied, "sell all that you have and distribute to the poor, and you will have treasure in heaven"[14] Such disciplines are hard for most. The rich man turned away saddened.

But the requirements of earth spirituality are no less exacting. If sky religion requires subtractive disciplines, earth religion requires additive disciplines. If sky religion aims for enlightenment, earth religion aims for fulfillment, filling the soul with experience. Earth religion is relational, person to person, creating optimal conditions for all in the family, all who share the neighborhood, all persons in a community, all in human society. Earth religion works directly and tangibly with

Buddhist gateway figures with serpentine vine,
Patna Museum, India.

others we know to ameliorate suffering, to lift up those who have fallen by the wayside, to serve others working towards a good life for all our lives touch.

There are two kinds of compassion, cool and hot. Cool compassion is of sky, such as the Buddha illustrated, a contemplative compassion for all sentient beings. Hot compassion is of the earth, such as St. Francis illustrated, a direct, hands-on assistance for the person before you, here and now. I cannot and would not say which spirituality might be more profound or superior. The world is in desperate need of both. It is important then, as the Bardo traditions of Tibet practice, to travel both ways on the spine of the Archetype of the Spirit, toward sky and toward earth, integrating as you proceed, with the goal of human wholeness.[15]

What then of the equally important secondary polarity of sun and moon? Here we will need to keep in mind Newman's model discussed in Chapter Four as well as a picture of the Archetype of the Spirit as a revolving mobile. Everything is in motion. Sky revolves even as the cosmos, the galaxies, and the weather patterns of earth's atmosphere revolve. Earth herself revolves but at a much more confined pace. The revolutions of earth we cannot perceive when we are living within them. Sun revolves in its galactic pattern and seems to move in relationship to earth. In our scientific age we know actually that the revolutions of earth eclipse our view of the sun. In the archetype sun revolves from sky towards earth crossing through earth's sphere at about the third chakra and circling back outward towards sky. Moon we know revolves around the earth. In the archetype moon circles from earth towards sky crossing through sky's sphere at about the fifth chakra and then around inward towards earth again.

We noted in Chapter Four that it is in the secondary polarity of sun (ST) and moon (NF) that we find the least regulated forms of perception: dominant Si for ISTJ, dominant Se for ESTP, dominant Ni for INFJ and dominant Ne for ENFP. Likewise the judging functions in four types in the secondary polarity tend to be attached to perceiving to a lesser degree: dominant Ti for ISTP, dominant Te for ESTJ, dominant Fi for INFP and dominant Fe for ENFJ, meaning there is a level of intensity or independence in the judging functions that accentuates their characteristics in these four types. In a sense the eight function-attitudes in the secondary polarity are called into application and action in more specialized or intense ways. A quick glance at the Four Spiritualities Mandala will show each of these eight types in their interface with the adjacent earth and sky spiritualities. For some this may appear as a mark of instability but to me it appears nature has accentuated these eight function-attitudes as a goad to their differentiation for all types. In a way it brings into a type context the observation of the Hindu saint, Ramakrishna, that rather than dissolving all tastes into water he would rather experience each separately, to get fully acquainted with them. If it is salt, its saltiness. If it is sugar, its sweetness. Likewise each of these eight types brings one function-attitude unmistakably forward. It gives all a taste of something perhaps hidden within themselves, which must be differentiated in order to be assimilated in human wholeness.

In the context of the archetype then, earth (SF) and sky (NT) revolve by each other at the heart chakra. Sun (ST) and moon (NF) revolve through each other, making their unmistakable qualities accessible to all. In spiritual journeys along the spine of the archetype, the pilgrim will encounter every function-attitude thus discovering his or her kinship with all elements of their humanity.

Afternoon view from Elephant Mountain, Guilin, China.

CHAPTER SIX

SPIRITUAL POISE

Spiritual poise involves the integration of the Archetype of the Spirit into a wholeness of the self, mediated by the presence of a balanced consciousness. Originally projected onto cosmic forms we must "see" the Archetype of the Spirit in its internal dynamics. The personality will be captained by one of the four aspects of the Archetype (cognitive function pairs) with the other three brought into play and affirmed. Essential is an accommodation of mystical experience with the ethical. Most important for our time in the twenty-first century will be a critical but compassionate appreciation for the fragile and tenuous emergence from the collective of individual consciousness itself.

It may be significant that every motif of the Archetype of the Spirit moves counterclockwise. In the everyday we keep track of time by watching the hands move in a clockwise direction as sun dial shadows once moved. In the passage of the seasons we trace them on the calendar in a clockwise direction, spring in the east, then summer in the south, fall in the west and winter to the north. The everyday and routinized move clockwise. To awaken to spiritual dimensions we must halt the spell of the ordinary and reverse direction. John Giannini calls counterclockwise "the 'sinister' chaotic dark side, which is the condition of creativity."[1] Thus sky gives rise to sun and earth to moon. Our spirituality is not all "sweetness and light." We must experience both the depths and the heights to come into a spiritual wholeness. We must awaken from the trance of the ordinary into a world of counter realities.

Often seated Buddhas transmit this motion as the Buddha's right or solar hand can be placed in the boon direction touching the lotus upon which he is seated. The lotus represents the mother earth goddess rooted in the dark rich recesses beneath the waters. The Buddha's left hand reaches out towards sky, the sign of blessing, a lunar gesture. In the stillness of the Buddha's meditation, a form of spiritual poise, a powerful energy moves counterclockwise.[2]

There was a time when this language of our Archetype was "read" nonverbally and from the unconscious. Like the phenomenon of 'body language' it was just there in the collective. No one took us by the hand and explained it to us. It was an integral

Step Pyramid, Saquara, Egypt, designed by Imhotep, viewed from the north. Shown are six steps above the subterranean chambers beneath. To the left of the picture is the Nile River valley, to the right a thousand miles of desert. Pictured also is the author's travel companion and wife, Eleanor.

experienced meaning in our participation. In a "state of nature" there was no individual responsibility, only a collective response. There was no Farmer's Almanac to inform us it was the evening for the full moon celebration. We just started chanting when darkness fell. The stories were enacted. The gratitude was expressed. So too was sky revered, the sun welcomed, and mother earth thanked. The Archetype of the Spirit in primeval times was projected onto the cosmic system. Sky was father, sun was son, earth was mother, moon was daughter. The dynamics of the workings of this archetype as a whole, the balancing, the compensating, was all unconscious. In crisis, solutions would erupt from the unconscious into a collective response. Only with the rise of extended human consciousness and of a sense of "I" as a separate individual, did we need to worry about responsibility. With individual

TOP LEFT: *Asklepios (Aesculapius), Greek god of healing, Epidauros, Greece.* TOP RIGHT: *Ruins of Epidauros in Greece, a gentle place of healing sacred to the god, Asklepios.* BELOW: *Sleeping Goddess from the Hypogeum, Malta.*

Focal point of a chapel on the campus of the Roman Catholic Catechetical and Liturgical Center in Bangalore, India, features a seven chakra altar with Christ placed at the fourth or Heart chakra. The medallion is known as "Christ the guru with disciple."

decisions, with responsibility, we see the emergence of human freedom.

With the advent of primary civilizations we can see the first terrors of responsibility for some in society, an occasional priest, or scribe, a poet among the nobility, a prophet out on the margins. In time elaborate state religious practices made explicit required behavior that before was simply done because it was what one did. Ritual procedures and social codes were written down because people were forgetting and reinventing for themselves what to celebrate. They had followed the great projections of the archetype into sky, sun, earth, moon. But when the individual emerged apart from the collective, unique and self conscious, then the problem of conformity was compounded. When projections into nature are withdrawn, nature can no longer take care of us, for the archetype must be understood in its real location all along, within the psyche itself. Sky, sun, earth, moon, are within us all.

It is thought that the great cities of the Indus Valley starved to death. Perhaps it was a sustained famine or a disease pandemic that exhausted the resilience of the people. Perhaps it was a work stoppage in the fields, a world weariness where order was so complete life was squeezed out.[3] We do know from coins and seals that in that time yoga was first practiced. For one thing the lotus posture expends the least energy needed to sustain life. On the other hand when life is most overwhelmed by circumstances beyond the individual's control there arises a great longing to awaken the essence within. Turning completely to internal reflective awareness yogis began opening the chakras, from earth to sky, invoking the energies of Ida and Pingala.

Meanwhile, the great architect, Imhotep, designed and supervised construction of the Step Pyramid at Saqqara, Egypt. Placed upon a flat desert plateau above the Nile its profile is six great steps, with a chamber below in earth and a flat crown for sky. In 1991 I stood in the sand to the north and faced south just in time to see the January sun burst a noon radiance across the summit flowing gold down its sides. Eventually Imhotep came to be known as a healing god.

His cousin, Asklepios in Greece, presided in Epidaurus where those distressed with dis-ease would journey to be healed. There was a steep path leading from the sea to a peaceful valley of pines surrounded by gentle hills. The compound for healing consisted in low buildings arranged around the courtyard of serpents and presided over by white robed priests who worked at night. One can imagine the moon bathing this valley in gentle light for the interpretation of dreams.

Earth (SF), sky (NT), sun (ST), moon (NF), are embodied within. One will lead this vulnerable and mortal being, differentiated in consciousness at the center in that hologram-like feature we call the ego. In the vicissitudes of both success and failure the other three elements of the archetype will make their presence felt. The ego thinks it knows the self, but the self is so much greater, and mostly unconscious. When things get too out of balance that which is not conscious in the archetype (and in other archetypes of the unconscious) can unsettle and overwhelm that which is. Resistance is futile. All we can hope for is to learn from our experiences, to concentrate upon realizing a higher order of balance than what went before. If the melodies of known chakras are in tune we can feel alive and well for a time. Life never rests and even in deep meditation the energies of boon and blessing circulate in the world.

Taoists find the origins of life in "original spirit," a kind of mystic soup out of which bubbles seem to free themselves from the surface riding for awhile as cohering entities.[4] That is something like the self, carrying within—actually being within— the soup itself or the collective unconscious. From that unconscious in turn come what Jung called complexes, one of which is a congeries of experiences, past, present and future, focusing enough to give a virtual center or ego. This wonderful omni-sequencing, omni-processing, but tiny portion of the self we know as consciousness is constantly shifting as the spotlight of consciousness somewhere in the lower regions of the brain brings into focus new experiences and we revisit and reinterpret a barrage of images or representations needed at any given moment.[5] With frequent revisiting of the spotlight, really reconstituting experience, consciousness becomes familiar, congenial, more spacious for our emergence as spiritual beings. The great task of living, its very purpose, was given us by Socrates: "Know thyself."

One of the most profound experiences of my life was a visit to the Hypogeum in Malta. It is deep underground in mother earth, several rooms carved round by Paleolithic people for the sleeping goddess. Ordinarily climbing down a spiral ladder into a deep confined space would render me rather apprehensive but here I felt completely at home. It was warm and affirming, holding me in its spell. Mother nature was complete there. Hewers of stone upon stone were wholly held within her embrace. There was no need of a Socrates there nor any chance of one appearing.

When we experience a complete at-homeness or what Damasio calls homeostasis or a state of well-being[6] we know the capacity for that experience is within us. Earth is within us as is sky, sun and moon. We are suited for life here on this planet. Our first task then is to bring ourselves into the reality of the presence of the Archetype of the Spirit within us and to come to recognize the movement of its aspects when life is out of balance. When one aspect becomes harmfully lopsided another, perhaps in dreams or in a time of conscious confusion, will assert itself in compensation. It is one thing to be overwhelmed by the components within us and quite another to recognize and be receptive of their energies and able to integrate them in an ongoing uniqueness of consciousness. We need a formula not of repression but of an accommodation of energies when they appear in dreams, fantasies, moods or impulses before the conscious personality (NT, SF, ST, or NF) is overwhelmed and "beside itself" in crisis or chaos.[7]

In a condition of spiritual poise the question of "Who am I?" or "What is my self?" will be balanced if not resolved. Attention will shift to "How or when do I know I am right?" When the self becomes manageable for the most part and we become reasonably comfortable in its ever changing and reconfiguring integrity, we turn again to a consideration of the collective in which we participate but towards which we now have become competently apart and free, voluntarily and selectively entering into its workings. Society is born of the earth, its norms arise from earth, its members variously within or beside its spell. If one's dominant and auxiliary functions are sensing and feeling (SF) the primary task has been to bring in sky (NT) so that one can freely participate as an individuated being rather than living entranced by mother earth. If one's dominant and auxiliary functions are intuiting and thinking (NT) the opposite task awaits, to integrate earth (SF) sufficiently that the tangible relationships of society can be rich and engaging rather than chaotic and strange. An ethical life requires inner balance if we are to do more good than harm with our lives. Likewise in the secondary polarity we work for a balance (not a stasis) between ST and NF, but in a context that may not ignore possible imbalances in the earth and sky polarities as well.

It is in this context we can begin to understand the enigmatic words of Jesus, "I speak in the world, even as I am not of the world."[8] He also said to his disciples, "You are not of the world, but I chose you out of the world[9] This appears to me as a call for sky perspective. In his prayer he rounds out his perspective at the heart chakra in his home (NF) spirituality:

> The glory which thou hast given me I have given to them, that they may be one even as we are one, I in them and thou in me, that they may become perfectly one, so that the world may know that thou hast sent me and hast loved them even as thou hast loved me.[10]

For such blasphemy of course he was crucified.[11]

When Lao Tzu had delivered his *Tao te Ching* he left society at the western gate. His exit was surely more gentle but just as complete. Both in their contexts and in their uniqueness delivered a boon and a blessing to all of us who follow. The message of our mortality and what we can accomplish in the interim is rhythmically summarized in Krishna's message to the warrior, Arjuna:

> Some say this Atman
> Is slain, and others
> Call It the slayer:
> They know nothing.

How can It slay
Or who shall slay It?

Know this Atman
Unborn, undying,
Never ceasing,
Never beginning,
Deathless, birthless,
Unchanging for ever.
How can It die
The death of the body?

Knowing It birthless,
Knowing It deathless,
Knowing It endless,
For ever unchanging,
Dream not you do
The deed of the killer,
Dream not the power
Is yours to command it.

Worn-out garments
Are shed by the body:
Worn-out bodies
Are shed by the dweller

Within the body.
New bodies are donned
By the dweller, like garments.

Not wounded by weapons,
Not burned by fire,
Not dried by the wind,
Not wetted by water:
Such is the Atman,
Not dried, not wetted,
Not burned, not wounded,
Innermost element
Everywhere, always,

Being of beings,
Changeless, eternal,
For ever and ever.[12]

With this awareness Arjuna would engage in mortal battle with the enemy. Leaving aside the theology of "atman" we can experience ourselves as nature, but nature as a flowing conjuries of influences through and including us, and in which nature's voice or experiential states of oneness may give rise to sublime self consciousness, that is a consciousness without boundaries between itself and all else.

The interaction of mystical continuity and ethical engagement is key for spiritual poise. As we withdrew our projections of the Archetype from the cosmos back into the workings of the psyche it then became imperative to make its workings accessible at least in bold outline to consciousness. Every individual must, in this sense, answer the call "out of the world" to truly engage with the world in human freedom. We must learn, individual by individual, "to think for ourselves," i.e. to become free beings.

To enter our freedom is to initiate a responsible participation. The whole Enlightenment project in the West of liberty and human rights arises from this juncture. We are born with "certain unalienable rights, to life, liberty and the pursuit of happiness." Such a birthright is not in nature; it is of sky. It is a creation of the human mind, rising as metaphoric experience through the seven chakras, until it bursts through in a brilliance of world-embracing affirmation. José Ortega y Gasset calls it "anti natural:"

> Liberal democracy carries to the extreme the determination to have consideration for one's neighbor. Liberalism is the supreme form of generosity; it is the right which the majority concedes to minorities and hence it is the noblest cry that has ever resounded in this planet. It announces the determination to share existence with the enemy; more than that, with an enemy which is weak. It was incredible that the human species should have arrived at so noble an attitude, so paradoxical, so refined, so acrobatic, so anti natural. Hence, it is not to be wondered at that this same humanity should soon appear anxious to get rid of it. It is a discipline too difficult and complex to take firm root on earth.[13]

In coming into our freedom, however tentative and sparsely manifest, we may well have discovered our purpose on the planet. We are, after all, the planet's self-awareness, its celebration, its voice.

Evil then has to do with regression towards a "state of nature," to abandon sky, to

Student art work at Shantiniketan (Place of Peace), Tagore's ashram and school, India.
This work shows the unconscious influences of the archetype as they appear, left to right,
a seven fold 'ladder' to a radiance, a sevenfold ascent of plant (rooted in earth) to bird,
and at right a plant image with birds in its upper limbs.

ignore the mediations of sun and moon, to abandon any human perspectives upon earth, disappearing into the Garden of Eden before the eating of the fruit of the tree of knowledge of good and evil. There are many who still long for a primeval and pre-conscious state before individuation outside the collective. They long for an unconscious obedience to the powers of the world. "Take care of me." Nothing short of a planetary holocaust would once again make this possible.

Good, the opposite polarity, has something to do with a widening of perspectives and a deepening of access for consciousness in mediating energies of the unconscious. Overcoming embeddedness in the local releases explosive energies of social chaos. But without perspective we languish in dependence and cannot enter freely and fully into our interdependence as planetary citizens. To manage the transition we must develop in ourselves wider visions (NT), new and reforming models of a larger order (ST), humane ideals for diverse relations (NF), always embodied in support and nurture for all those our lives touch at the hearthsides of our living (SF).

Each child born to his or her planetary human inheritance must begin from the preconscious ground, must differentiate their consciousness in the four functions (S, N,

T, F), in the two attitudes (E, I), living in the archetypal soup of the unconscious ("original spirit"). As the child matures it comes into its conscious powers, manifesting in varying degrees the qualities of earth (SF), sky (NT), sun (ST) and moon (NF). First perspectives will be intensely local but with the goal of bringing their unique individuated person into a global consciousness and embrace. A person must rise from self-centered, to tradition/local centered, to becoming a self-forming individual, and from there to a multi-affirming and global-affiliating participation in planetary life.[14] Nothing short of this embrace can be tenable as a goal in this age.[15] And yet when falling short of a spiritual poise few have an inkling (1) of any imperative to realize a larger conscious wholeness, or (2) why it is so critical at this time.

It cannot be emphasized enough how tenuous a higher consciousness is, how recently it dawned in the four billion year history of earth, and how in every generation, in every new born infant this fragile defining human quality must be born anew. The child discovers that the world exists and further that in that world the child exists. Carl Jung announced this ever recurring and epical discovery in the context of hero mythology:

> The hero's main feat is to overcome the monster of darkness: it is the long hoped-for and expected triumph of consciousness over the unconscious . . . The coming of consciousness was probably the

Jewish Memorial. Dachau, Munich Germany. Note the seven branch menorah and the sky and earth triangles forming a Star of David at the heart chakra.

Portal of the Virgin, Notre Dame of Paris. Note Adam and Eve with the serpent below. Paris, France.

most tremendous experience of primeval times, for with it a world came into being whose existence no one had suspected before. "And God said, 'Let there be light'" is the projection of that immemorial experience of the separation of consciousness from the unconscious.[16]

When I was young I remember my mother roundly criticized the *Genesis* story as light was "created" on the first day while the sun and moon came along on the fourth day. Her error was a misplaced concreteness. This and all the great stories of our human nature are not empirical scientific treatises. And certainly as the next verse makes clear it is limited even to an age when land peoples believed earth was flat and "heaven" was in a finite place "up there."[17] Jung rightly transforms the reality of the story. Out of the depths within ourselves earth "sees." And more: we perceive ourselves as the source of that light. Through individual perception a cosmos is created, is brought into conscious focus, the waters are parted and replacing darkness and void, out of the primal chaos (Tiamat) our world comes into being. To read the story literally is to project qualities within ourselves out onto the sky, the sun, moon and earth. It has taken millennia to bring these projections back in, even now ever so tentatively. We cannot attain a spiritual poise in our time unless the entire

Window from Adam, Eve and the tree, to the crucifixion. Basilica Saint-Nazaire, Carcassonne, France.

archetype is processed as an internal dynamic balance, individual by individual, rather than as a collective process.

All human stories are our stories. They have sustained our emergence for tens of generations. Now is the era when they must be brought from the outside to the inside. We now require in-sight, "Let there be light" fulfilled! A survey of the history of an English language vocabulary of consciousness is sobering. "Consciousness" as a word first came into use in the seventeenth century. The words "individual" or "individuation" can be pushed back also into the seventeenth century. The word "person" for a long time held the original meaning of "persona," putting on a mask or playing a part. It and "parson" was long a designation for a separate entity or subject of the realm, a social entity with certain rights and duties playing a part until, again

Lion devouring human, beside main entrance,
Cathedral, Assisi, Italy.

the seventeenth century, the aspect of personality came into infrequent usage. "Self"
is an early word going back a millennium. However, as a reference to an intrinsic
separate reality metaphorically a soul or mind ascending from the body, we once again
find it emerging into usage in the seventeenth century or very late sixteenth. We tend
to assume that a form of consciousness we know has always been. And of course there
are examples back perhaps as far as three thousand years who experienced something
akin to what we know. It having always been a human potentiality, a higher autobiographical consciousness occasionally surfaced proving yet again how tenuous is its
existence. The professions of psychotherapy and analytical psychology were called
into existence when enough people were living on the thin edge of consciousness
crying for help and reassurance. The example of King Saul (*I Samuel*) and the terrors
of his dawning but fragile consciousness were not uncommon even into the twentieth
century![18]

In preconscious ages spirituality as we have seen was projected outward to cosmic
phenomena, earth, sky, sun, moon, and worked through in the collective. Projections
were made to other archetypes, the heroes, saviors, tricksters, demons. When
consciousness was differentiated spiritual disciplines were required to calm the terrors
and the dangers of ego inflation, to balance the self towards wholeness. Even today
the great majority are fortunate if they can differentiate and develop healthy
dominant and auxiliary functions and not be overwhelmed by eruptions of the fourth
or inferior function (sometimes referred to as carrying the anima/animus archetype)
or other complexes from the unconscious. Consider the tasks of meditative
disciplines, to reduce an egocentric orientation, to calm and contain the inflated ego.
When such disciplines turn into a drive to submerge the ego again into an
unconscious escape they cease to be spiritual exercises and can only be considered as
regressions. Meditation should calm but not extinguish the ego.

I had long wondered why meditative disciplines needed to take years and
decades, until I perceived them (at least in part) as exercises of type development. In
the midst of the challenges of life what is likely to happen when the ego is stilled is
an eruption of the inferior function pouncing into the breach. Consider for example
a person with introverted feeling and extraverted intuition (INFP). When the
dominant function (Fi) is quieted along with the auxiliary function (Ne) what would
then become the "captain of the ship" of personality (to use Isabel Briggs-Myers'
metaphor)? Very likely it would be the inferior function (Te) commandeering the
tertiary function (Si) as its auxiliary. But this opposite constellation (ST), being
weaker and less reliable (for an INFP), life would become unsteady, even chaotic. In
panic all calm is broken and the person restores the dominance of their native
intuitive feeling (NF). Such terror at "losing oneself" (really losing one's ego control,
not oneself), needs the presence of a strong guide, the reassurance of a spiritual

director, or guru, teacher, or close-knit community. Otherwise the meditative practice becomes too disturbing to continue. The fierce lions, demons, warriors that guard the gates of Buddhist temples in China or Catholic cathedrals in Europe are there advisedly! And if after years of practice (to refer to our example INFP) the first four function-attitudes (Fi, Ne, Si, Te) are calmed, then there are four more which can be equally confrontational (Fe, Ni, Se, Ti) in the meditative aspect of the journey towards wholeness, spiritual poise (see earlier FIGURE 5, chapter 1).

It is at this point in our spiritual development that we must return home for perspective. Put simply, every deepening towards earth, every adventure towards sky, brings us into a more complete sympathy for all humankind who journey with us on this planet. That is what this brief mortal life is for, to bring the world closer to the "kingdom of heaven on earth."[19] Every step by us as individuals towards spiritual poise makes it more incumbent upon us to help others, to bring society into a balance. This it seems to me is the intention of the four great Maha Bodhisattvas of the *Lotus Sutra* (counterclockwise from sky):

> (1) the Bodhisattva of Boundless Conduct (NT)
> "However limitless the Buddha's teachings are, I vow to study them."

Rissho Kosei-Kai Buddhist altar arrangement. Surrounding Sakyamuni Buddha on the altar piece are Maitreya Bodhisattva in the sky position with the four mahabodhisattvas, of Boundless Conduct (NT), Steadfast Conduct (ST), Pure Conduct (SF) and Eminent Conduct (NF).

Collosal Merciful Buddha, Popchusa Temple,
South Korea, an Amida pure land site.
Hands are in the boon and blessing positions.

*Obelisk, Heliopolis, Egypt. The last remaining of seven, the others
in Istanbul, Rome, Paris, London and New York and another missing.*

(2) the Bodhisattva of Steadfast Conduct (ST)
"However innumerable living beings are, I vow to save them."
(3) the Bodhisattva of Pure Conduct (SF)
"However inexhaustible the passions are, I vow to extinguish them."
(4) the Bodhisattva of Eminent Conduct (NF)
"However infinite the Buddha-truth is, I vow to attain it."[20]

Whether by subtractive or additive spiritual strategies, whether through enlightenment or fulfillment, well-individuated spiritual development brings us through these four gates to our human wholeness.

Spiritual poise arises in us as we center upon the Mandala where all five elements of the Archetype of the Spirit may work within the balanced self. From north and west, south and east, powerful elements of spiritual consciousness converge at the tree of life, the heart of our living. Sky consciousness within us can be brought in further so as to overlap with earth rising. Sun and moon circulate through, in such a circuit that sun vision and order becomes a grandfatherly elder presence and the moon idealist circles to become Sophia in the soul. Poise comes in the serpent spirals of ever changing perspectives as all sectors of the archetype work their health into the whole. We come to live in the multitude of perspectives of human wellbeing. We are of them and they in us. We are cosmic beings who know earth as our home. Experienced subjectively it is known objectively. Our consciousness together with our larger self are at once engaged and at peace, living at the threshold of the unknown.

More than four thousand years ago one of the great temple centers of our humanity was founded at Heliopolis in Middle Egypt. The Archetype of the Spirit in various permutations was present there. I visited it in 1991 and found one remaining evidence of its glory, a magnificent solar obelisk where once there had been seven. Since the demise of ancient Egyptian power after two thousand years, successive empires have taken obelisks away, one to the Byzantine capital, now Istanbul; one to the eternal city, Rome; one to Paris; one to London and a sixth to New York. I have ever since wondered at the fate of the seventh obelisk. Perhaps like Akhenaton's temple at Karnak it was used as rubble to build the temple of a rival god. Perhaps it sank beneath the waters in the hull of a great ship. Or I like to muse it led a phantom existence in dream and story. I think of it as embodied in all who seek a spiritual poise. In its omnipresent passages through life, it could save the world!

Trees and sky, Crystal River Archeological State Park, Florida.

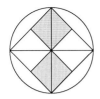

Earth, Sky, Sun, Moon and Tree

EARTH

To kneel upon the soft soil,
to work loam until it receives the seed;
we can feel the goodness.
We can smell it in the moist ground.
We can know the goodness
as the seed splits, sends up its yellow blade,
turns in the light for green transformations,
restores goodness to the nourishing root.

Earth is the mother of life.
She responds to the presence of light,
the collaboration of human hands.
Her powers are great
in the ceaseless cycles of moisture and soil,
of fires at the center of shifting continents,
of her seasons of creation and regeneration.
She replenishes, she sustains, she nurtures.

A living cycle of the seasons keeps time
as surely as heartbeat follows upon heartbeat.
Summer grows green, replenishes the generations
        of flora and fauna abundant.
Autumn gives harvest of plenty
        as seed sinks into the receiving soil.
Winter brings in a fallow time

forcing closure to one cycle, preparing for the next.
Spring unleashes blossoms and bees,
      pushes trillions of green leaves into the light.

But we have found fossils of fern in Greenland,
where glaciers of ice now reign,
And remains of glaciers in New England
where green trees and sweet berries now grow.
Volcanoes have prevented summers
and carbon emissions have prevented winters.
Deserts expand where jungles once grew
and rolling fields of wheat where dust once blew.

Civilization has grown upon the earth
transforming landscapes for human habitation.
Rivers are diverted to water fields,
mountains are carried to fill valleys.
The air is brown over cities.
Frogs are born deformed in our lakes.
The blood in our bodies turns toxic.
Can we imagine all compensations
as mother earth responds to our deprivations?

Caverns of earth open, giving birth to rivers.
Pores of earth open to sponsor seeds of life.
From steaming pools prokaryote and eukaryote cells emerged.
The sea brought forth kelp, crawlers and swimmers.
Ferns, flowers, amphibians, reptiles diverged upon her continents.
Birds took wing from her nests, and warm blooded mammals.
Primates, then humans came to live, one with another.
Every living being, for better or worse, interacts in relationship
      with all other living beings in communal interdependence.

Now earth can play games and wage wars
      of slaughter and extinction.
Now earth can speak of meanings
      and the purpose of life.
Now earth can chronicle its own emergence
      beaming messages to imagined kindred planets.

Now earth can sing celebrations of itself
    and pulse with electric grids.
Earth has become the artifact of life
    or it may return to night for another dawn of consciousness.
Mother earth which nurtures all
    is the womb and doom of every living offspring.
Every child is her child;
    every elder is received into her cycles of everlasting care.

SKY

Birds of flight do not rest long.
They must take to wing
out from the safety of trees,
out in the realm of soaring hawks,
    eagles, gulls, carrion crows,
out in the currents of wind,
out in the open invisible,
in all directions blue, flowing white,
the broad curve of earth below.

When light fades to dark
a canopy of stars is revealed,
glorious sparkling diamonds of light.
Familiar formations emerge
to the north, to the south, west and east,
triangulations for navigations of mind,
adventures of imagination.
Are there messages of human purpose there?
Are there premonitions of turning points?
    hinges of history?

Breathe deeply of air invisible,
restorer of life.
Breathe in regular rhythm,
filling, emptying.
The oneness flows
within—among—beyond,
Divine spirit renewing,

invisible—indivisible—eternal presence.
A part of us is a part of all,
emptying into the great void of space,
the light everlasting.

Each of us must die alone
    to be absorbed in a great illumination.
Each of us must understand alone
    the great patterns of integration.
Alone, each of us must wrestle with the demons,
    the saboteurs of concentration.
Each of us, alone, must enter the wilderness,
    barren places of desolation.
For out of death comes life
    a seering rebirth of vision.
Out of the wilderness is born justice
    and the sweet taste of wisdom.

Few journey under sky,
    live in the wastelands of desert
    in silence and the brightness of night.
Few leave landmarks of home
    to sail upon vast waters
    out from all but ruminations of mind.
Few climb to mountain tops
    discarding all possessions along the way.
Jesus, the Buddha, Mohammed, Lao Tzu,
    traveled through clouds,
    opening purviews of enlightenment.
Blessed are the few who enter
    realms of simple light,
    for theirs is the "kingdom of heaven."

The serpent of consciousness expands
    opening centers increasingly sublime.
For a moment life opens to its infinitude,
    suspends its body, its self, in pure mind.
Galaxies whirl into the first moment prior to creation
    in the white void of silence.

SUN

Sun stirs sky into whirlwinds
destroying trees, homes and habitats,
rising dust into tornadoes
and lakes into water spouts,
tearing, leveling, with chaos bringing order.

So intense is the presence of summer sun
wax melts into pools,
skin blisters and blackens into melanomas
and clay stiffens and cracks
releasing its moisture into the winds of sky.
Sunstroke threatens the callous and impatient.
Do not ignore sun's light, sun's heat!

Winter sun is cold, unforgiving,
a judgment upon the world weary,
receding, warning of deprivations
for all who do not engage life,
all who in prosperity do not anticipate barron times,
or squander inner powers to create new worlds.

Lawgivers descend from pivotal conferences
before the burning bush on Mount Sinai,
or atop ziggurats in the presence of winged messengers,
lining out the way we should walk,
how the world coheres
when each one of us plays our appointed part.

Prophets of righteousness arise,
ascend with prophesies of doom:
unless we change our reifyed ways,
unless we live in fealty to truth
unless we honor the received traditions,
fulfill the vision of "a new commonwealth
set upon a hill," "a glorious golden city."

From the heavens come heroes

radiating golden halos.
Not of this world,
they enter to teach new pathways
illumined in glowing rays
of the paternal sun.

Heaven's light come down
to draw new pathways for the journey,
Heaven's urgency to show the way
that we may know the glorious goal of our work,
Heaven's warning and rescue
that we may find resolute pathways for our feet;
We act in the bright light of midday,
the zenith of the year,
that we may prevail, that life may live.

MOON

Through forest mists
in the darkness,
We look out past branches of oak
to the crescent moon.

Rounded but sharp pointed,
convex, its darker form faintly filling,
maiden moon is building,
patiently enlarging the purview of her presence.

She ascends faithfully each evening
in the East, waxing ever larger,
maiden to mother growing,
mother and child rising
(Isis and Horus, Mary and Jesus)
to her fullfillment.

Her consort is the prancing bull
emerging from the dark,
lifting his horn to the East,
then glaring straight in, eyes wide, nostrils flared,
clouds drifting across his gaze,

then lifting his horn to the waning West,
fading into the darkness of the night.

Dusk to dawn is the poet's muse
becoming intense in the silent night.
When others sleep the poet awakes,
writing with candle flame in silent chamber
gazing out through open window to the night
with pale lit landscape beneath
ascending reflections in a trail of blue light.

A thirteen-fold cycle of worship
welcomes full moons rising orange in the East.
Out of the great sea, sending tides before it,
the orb rises in a glistening trail of waves.
Bringing to the hillside tribe a hushed silence,
she rises, benevolent, filling the world.
She comes pervasive, powerfully pregnant,
pouring from the wounds of compassion
boons abundant for a world longing for life
nurtured into wholeness, meaning, assurance.

The wailing invocation rises
in pulsing rhythm of lament
of hunger in all empty places
for her healing presence,
to draw energies from earth
into the great orbit of the living,
to grow in the communal body
a plenteous peace,
harmony in the heart.

Moon animates the silent spaces of life,
deep reflections upon the mind's mirrored waters,
fathomless, still, profound.
Moon restores to the restive spirit
a soul-full assurance, a resilience,
a patience gathering
giving life to life
that will endure for all time.

Through forest mists
in the pregnant darkness
we look out through branches of oak
to know the waxing and waning crescent
and a fullness awesome
assurance in the heart.

TREE

How tenuous and determined
are the claims of life upon our earth.

The first cry of baby sound
in delicate air;
How like the first motion of a cell
billions of years ago
in a bubble floating across a volcanic pool.

Vulnerable is our life
to narrow tolerances of degrees fahrenheit.
So vulnerable is our life
to loving care, hugging together against the cold,
reassuring attention to the dire needs of first dependence.

How tenuous and determined
are the claims of life upon our earth.

From deep origins in black cosmic soils
the Tree of Life emerges into light
raising its limbs to meet the energy of sky.
The Tree of Life branches
inward and outward
    growing deep roots
    growing lofty limbs.

Interdependent, ever-green, is the flow of life:
    sky to earth, earth to sky,
    light to limb, limb to root,
    root to limb, limb to light,
    light to green, green to dark

dark to green, green to light
Light and dark grow ever-green.

We grow in our limbs and our roots.
We stretch to anticipate new reachings ahead.
We stretch to understand through deep remembering.
We live where understanding and anticipations meet.
    We grow our roots to live.
    We grow our limbs to live.

As roots of our being stretch
    new insights rush to nourish us.
As limbs of our being stretch
    new possibilities light our days.
It is in our growing back and growing forward
  ⸌ that experience deepens.
    Life moves us and we move life.

How tenuous and determined
are the claims of life upon our earth.

First cry in the delicate air:
encircling arms reassure us.
How firmly rooted is life grounded in love.

Second cry in the delicate air:
brings forth intriguing echoes to explore.
We crawl and walk, test and play,
returning to loving arms
venturing to horizons of wonder and creation.

Life stretches us in its roots and limbs.
How fearsome but sustaining is the dark of nurture.
How blinding but alluring is the light of reaching.
First steps venture to the next form and shape of being,
first steps trusting the firm base of our advance.

How tenuous and determined
are the claims of life upon our earth.

Floral Medalion Design, Unitarian Church, Kovend, Romania.

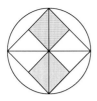

NOTES

CHAPTER ONE

1. Much has been made recently of so called "mirror neurons," which Antonio Damasio sees as activating mental images as if they came from within one's own body when actually they were perceived as objects outside. This doubtless had great value in our early years and can be a physiological basis for sympathy. Studies have been conducted using photographs depicting emotion where responses were accurate in identifying the emotions portrayed (see Damasio, Looking For Spinoza, pp. 116-118). George Lakoff identifies mirror neurons as a basis for empathy, "feeling what another feels." (see Lakoff, Whose Freedom, pp. 85-88.) If empathy, rather than sympathy or compassion, is inborn it is critical to heed the warnings of Edwin Friedman on its overuse and the risk of weakening individual responsibility, leadership and resistance to social pathogens.

2. Consciousness is of course more complex than any model of it. Jung's conclusions anticipate the entire new field of cognitive and neurological psychology. See for example the work of Antonio Damasio, George Lakoff, Patricia Churchland and others.

3. Taking in, perceiving, involves constantly updating body maps and reconstituting body maps (memory) of feelings and further emotional or body states which feelings apprehend. All perception is a responding to our own body's responses to itself and objects outside itself. "Higher" levels of cognition, perceiving and judging, rest on a vast universe of electric and chemical modulating activities of 100 billion or so neurons. Most of this activity of course is unconscious as consciousness is a small bubble riding on a large sea of the unconscious.

4. Carl G. Jung, *Psychological Types* (Princeton: Princeton University Press, 1971), p. 540. In his words:

    > I have been asked, almost accusingly, why I speak of four functions and not of more or fewer. That there are exactly four was a result I arrived at on purely empirical grounds. But as the following consideration will show, these four together produce a kind of totality. Sensation establishes what is actually present, thinking enables us to recognize its meaning, feeling tells us its value, and intuition points to possibilities as to whence it came and whither it is going in a given situation.

5. Isabel Briggs Myers, *Gifts Differing* (Palo Alto: Consulting Psychologists Press, 1980), pp. 17-25.

6. Jung, *Psychological Types.* p. 541.

7. Jung, *Psychological Types*, pp. 405-406.

8. John L. Giannini, *Compass of the Soul: Archetypal Guides to a Fuller Life* (Gainesville: Center for Applications of Psychological Type, 2004) p. 95ff.

9. Peter Tufts Richardson, *Four Spiritualities: A Psychology of Contemporary Spiritual Choice.* (Palo Alto: Davies-Black Publishing, 1996), p. 186.

10. Jung, *Psychological Types*, p. 541.

11. Leola Haas and Mark Hunziker, *Building Blocks of Personality Type* (Huntington Beach: Telos Publications, 2006), pp. 127-130. These oppositions can be directly seen in FIGURE 5, Function Attitudes Wheel.

12. Naomi L. Quenk, *Beside Ourselves: Our Hidden Personality in Everyday Life* (Palo Alto: CPP Books, 1993), p. 71.

13. John Beebe, *A New Model of Psychological Types* (Chicago: C. G. Jung Institute of Chicago, 1988), 5 Audio Tapes.

14. Anne Singer Harris, *Living With Paradox: An Introduction to Jungian Psychology* (Albany: Brooks/Cole Publishing, 1996), p. 67.

15. A rather striking example of the problem of believing you know your type when you have your four letters can be seen in the recent book, *The Cult of Personality* by Annie Murphy Paul. In three places, pp. 111,112,123, she gives examples of three types, ISTJ, INFP, ENFP. She explains them as "introverted-sensing-thinking-judging," "introverted-intuitive-feeling-perceiving," and

"extroverted-intuitive-feeling-perceiver" respectively (note the misspelling of extraverted). She thus shows a complete lack of awareness of type dynamics. Had she advanced beyond a labeling stance she would have described these types as introverted sensing with extraverted thinking, introverted feeling with extraverted intuition, and extraverted intuition with introverted feeling. In addition she shows no evidence of having considered the principles of type development nor the difference between a tool of discernment, the Myers-Briggs Type Indicator (MBTI™) which she calls a "test," and psychological type itself which is a portion of Jungian theory of the human self, type being a way of describing the differentiation of the conscious aspects of the self.

CHAPTER TWO

1. Carl G. Jung, "A Psychological Approach to the Dogma of the Trinity," in *Psychology and Religion: West and East* (New York: Bollingen Foundation, 1958), Vol. 11, p. 149n.

2. Angelo Spoto, *Jung's Typology in Perspective* (Wilmette: Chiron Publications, 1995), p. 92.

3. Walpola Rahula, *What the Buddha Taught* (New York: Grove Weidenfeld, 1959), pp. 16-28. See also Ananda Coomaraswamy, *Buddha and the Gospel of Buddhism* (New York: Harper & Row, 1916, 1964), pp. 90-93.

4. Peter Tufts Richardson, *Growing Your Spirituality* (Rockland, ME: Red Barn Publishing, 2001), pp. 81-95.

5. Carl G. Jung, *Answer to Job* (Princeton: Princeton University Press, 2002), p. xiv.

6. In Beijing, the Altar of Heaven has the square (earth) outside and the circle (sky) inside. Through the square are four magnificent gates at the cardinal points with walkways leading to ornate stairways and to the center of the circle i.e. the cross.

7. *Genesis* 1: 6-8.

8. David Hinton, trans., *Mencius* (Washington: Counterpoint, 1998), II: 4, 6; IV: 4; IX: 5. For a discussion of the influence of Confucian ideas on the emergence of democracy in the West, see H. G. Creel, *Confucius and the Chinese Way* (New York: Harper & Brothers, 1959), pp. 254-285.

9. The tree appears at the beginning and at the end, a mythological closure. However it was a major issue for early Christians given a literal understanding

of the passage, "Cursed is every one that hangeth on a tree." (*Deut.*21:23, *Gal.* 3:13). See Morton S. Enslin, *From Jesus to Christianity* (Boston: Beacon Press, 1964), pp. 18-19.

10. Carl G. Jung, *Psychology & Religion* (New Haven: Yale University Press, 1938), p. 76. See also pp. 63-82.

11. Carl G. Jung, *Answer to Job*, p. 85.

12. Carl G. Jung, *Mandala Symbolism* (Princeton: Princeton University Press, 1972), p. 73. For additional discussion of opposites united in the deity see, Jung's *Memories, Dreams, Reflections* (New York: Vintage Books, 1965), pp. 333-338, and of course Jung's *Answer to Job*.

13. Carl G. Jung, quoted in Jolande Jacobi & R. F. C. Hull, eds., *Psychological Reflections* (Princeton: Princeton University Press, 1973), p. 97. It cannot be emphasized enough how important Jung found oppositions in the self, the lifelong wrestling with elements of the unconscious rising to challenge the specializations of ego consciousness. This is in drastic contrast to those who would repress or replace such challenges with a sea of blissful tranquility. There is no shortcut to the contest of opposing elements of the self to a balanced resolution for awhile, not a suppression which cannot lead to wholeness. See for example David Tracey, *Jung and the New Age* (England: Brunner-Routledge, 2001).

CHAPTER THREE

1. Albert Schweitzer, *Out of My Life and Thought* (New York: New American Library, 1955), p. 124.

2. Barbara S. Miller, trans., *The Bhagavad Gita* (New York: Bantam Books, 1988), 5: 16, p. 59.

3. Margaret Fuller quoted in R. Buckminster Fuller, *Ideas and Integrities* (New York: Collier Books, 1963), p. 70.

4. William Ellery Channing, "Likeness to God," 1828 in *The Works of William E. Channing, D.D.* (Boston: James Munroe, 1843), Vol. III, pp. 233-234.

5. R. Buckminster Fuller, *Nine Chains to the Moon* (Carbondale: Southern Illinois University Press, 1963), p. 19.

6. P. Lal, trans., *Dhammapada* (New York: Farrar, Straus & Giroux, 1967), p. 45.

7. Thomas Merton, *The Seven Storey Mountain* (New York: New American Library, 1948), p. 314.

8. *Amos* (RSV), 5: 21-24.

9. Theodore Parker, *Experience as a Minister* (Boston: Rufus Leighton, 1859), p. 117.

10. Swami Nikhilananda, trans., *The Gospel of Sri Ramakrishna* (New York: Ramakrishna-Vivekananda Center, 1942), p. 565; and quoted in Solange LaMaitre, *Ramakrishna and the Vitality of Hinduism* (New York: Funk and Wagnalls, 1969), p. 166.

11. This popular hymn by the English Unitarian, Sarah Flower Adams, is found in many hymnals, for example, *Singing the Living Tradition* (Boston: Beacon Press, 1993), no. 87.

12. Abdullah Yusuf Ali, trans., *The Holy Qur-an* (Lahore: Sh. Muhammad Ashraf, 1969), XCIII: 6-8, p. 1752.

13. La ilaha illallah Muhammad-ur-Rasulullah. Abul A'La Mawdudi, *Towards Understanding Islam* (Delhi: Markazi Maktaba Islami, 1993), p. 86.

14. Allama Sir Abdullah Al-Mamun Al-Suhrawardy, trans., *The Sayings of Muhammad* (New York: Citadel Press, 1990), p. 53.

15. *Luke* 10: 38-42.

16. Mother Teresa, *Words to Love by. . .* (Notre Dame, IN: Ave Maria Press, 1995), p. 75.

17. *Matthew* 7:12; 22:38; 6:12.

18. *The Book of Common Prayer and Administration of the Sacraments and Other Rites and Ceremonies of the Church According to the Use of the Episcopal Church* (New York: Church Hymnal Corporation and the Seabury Press, 1977), p. 321.

19. Edward Everett Hale, *Sermons of the Winter* (Boston: J. Stilman Smith, 1893), pp. 141-142.

20. Edward Everett Hale, Jr., ed., *The Life and Letters of Edward Everett Hale* (Boston: Little Brown, 1917), p. 122.

21. Barbara S. Miller, ed., *The Bhagavad-Gita* (New York: Bantam Books, 1986), 3: 24, p. 44.

22. Roland H. Bainton, *Here I Stand: A Life of Martin Luther* (New York: New

American Library, 1950), p. 144.

23. *Hymns of the Spirit* (Boston: Beacon Press, 1937), No. 567 by Julia Ward Howe.

24. *The Practice of the Presence of God: Being Conversations and Letters of Brother Lawrence* (London: A. R. Mowbray, 1961).

25. M. K. Gandhi, *The Bhagavadgita* (New Delhi: Orient Paperbacks, 1980), p. 78.

26. Arthur Waley, trans., *Translations from the Chinese* (New York: Knopf, 1964), pp. 228-229.

27. Quoted in Joseph Campbell, *Power of Myth* (New York: Doubleday, 1988), p. 34.

28. Vincent B. Silliman, ed., *A Selection of Services for Special Occasions* (Boston: Unitarian Universalist Ministers Association, 1981), p. 51.

29. Ralph Waldo Emerson, "Self-Reliance" (1841) in *The Essays of Ralph Waldo Emerson* (New York: Heritage Press, 1934), P. 29.

30. Rainer Maria Rilke, *Letters to a Young Poet*, Stephen Mitchell, trans. (New York: Vintage Books, 1986), p. 9.

31. Loren Eiseley, *The Firmament of Time* (New York: Atheneum, 1960), pp. 181-182.

32. D. C. Lau, trans., *Lao Tzu: Tao Te Ching* (Baltimore: Penguin Books, 1963), no. 25, p. 82.

33. William Blake, "Auguries of Innocence" (1805).

34. Thomas Merton, trans., *The Way of Chuang Tzu* (New York: New Directions, 1965), p. 65.

35. Rabindranath Tagore, *Religion of Man* (Boston: Beacon Press, 1961), pp. 93-94.

36. *John* (RSV) 3: 7-9.

37. *John* 19: 38-41.

38. *Matthew* 5: 1-12.

39. *Luke* 18:25.

40. *Thomas*, Saying 112, in Marvin W. Meyer, trans., *The Secret Teachings of Jesus: Four Gnostic Gospels* (New York: Random House, 1984), p. 51.

41. Starhawk (Miriam Simos), *Dreaming the Dark* (Boston: Beacon Press, 1982), p. 92.

42. Walt Whitman, "Song of the Open Road" and "One's-Self I Sing" in Maxwell

Geismar, ed., *The Whitman Reader* (New York, Pocket Books, 1955), pp. 86, 1.

43. For a summary of Philosophia see Wilfred C. Smith, "Philosophia as One of the Religious Traditions of Humankind," in *Modern Culture from a Comparative Perspective* (Albany: State University of New York Press, 1997), pp. 19-49; and Huston Smith, "Western Philosophy as a Great Religion," in *Essays on World Religion* (New York: Paragon House, 1995), pp. 205-223.

CHAPTER FOUR

1. Tennyson's poem, "Ulysses," is a classic of sea faring traditions. It continues:

   > Yet all experience is an arch where through
   > Gleams that untraveled world whose margin fades
   > Forever and forever when I move.
   > . . . . Come, my friends,
   > 'Tis not too late to seek a newer world.
   > Push off, and sitting well in order smite
   > The sounding furrows; for my purpose holds
   > To sail beyond the sunset, and the baths
   > Of all the western stars, until I die.

2. *Psalm 8: 3-8.*

3. *Psalm 22: 1-2.* (see also Matthew 27:46)

4. R. Buckminster Fuller, *Synergetics: Explorations in the Geometry of Thinking* (New York: MacMillan Publishing, 1975), Vol. 1, pp. 749-751. See also Fuller's *Critical Path* (New York: St. Martin's Press, 1981), pp. 11-59.

5. Joseph Campbell, *Transformations of Myth Through Time* (New York: Harper & Row, pp. 68-71. See also: Cyrus H. Gordon, *Before the Bible* (New York: Harper & Row, 1962), p. 279; Henri Frankfort et al, *Before Philosophy* (Baltimore: Penguin Books, 1963), pp. 222-223; James Bailey, *The God-Kings & The Titans* (New York: St. Martin's Press, 1973), pp. 106-115.

6. *Exodus 34: 29.*

7. Apollo is a composite god with origins as a god of Shepherds, of music and poetry, of the qualities of Shamesh, a sun god, of law and administration, of light and of healing. He gradually preempted the characteristics of Helios the Greek sun god. He was born of the goddess Leda in Delos but Delphi became

his chief center with the defeat of Python, a dragon defending the navel of the earth. His son was Asklepios, the god of medicine whose primary center was at Epidaurus. The stool of Plataea at Delphi had three intertwined serpents for its spine. Asklepios of course had the staff with entwined serpent.

8. Hinton, *Mencius* II: 6.

9. The crescent moon and star, Venus, is the central symbol of Islam found on minarets, domes and rooftops.

10. Ralph Waldo Emerson, "The Poet" *Essays: Second Series* (New York: The Heritage Press, 1934), pp. 148-165. This is a strong theme around the globe, for example, see also Rabindranath Tagore, *The Religion of Man* (Boston: Beacon Press, 1931), Chapter VI, "The Vision," pp. 90-108; E. J. Applewhite, *Cosmic Fishing* (New York: MacMillan Publishing Co.), pp. 57-61; Kenneth L. Patton, *A Religion for One World* (Boston: Beacon Press & Meeting House Press, 1964), Chapter 8, pp. 125-134.

11. *Isaiah* 53.

12. A remarkable example of the lunar goddess with vivid detailed description of her appearance can be found in Apuleius' classic Roman novel, *The Golden Ass*, Robert Graves, trans. (New York: The Pocket Library, 1955), Chapter 17, pp. 230-240.

13. Roger T. Ames and David L. Hall, *Daodejing:"Making This Life Significant": A Philosophical Translation* (New York: Ballantine Books, 2003), Chapter 7, p. 86.

14. James Newman, *A Cognitive Perspective on Jungian Typology* (Gainesville: Center for the Application of Psychological Type, 1990). See also, James Newman, *Cognition and Consciousness*, set of three tapes and accompanying guide book. (Gainesville: Center for Applications of Psychological Type, 1990); James B. Newman, *Hemisphere Specialization and Jungian Typology: Evidence for a Relationship* (PhD thesis: Pacific Graduate School of Psychology, 1984).

15. Among the passages in Damasio's works which illumine the feeling function and hemispheric specialization are *Descartes' Error*, pp. xiv-xvi, 17-19, 39, 51, 61-70, 78, 132-140, 143, 145, 149-154, 158-159; *The Feeling of What Happens*, 39, 41, 108-111, 156, 187, 209-212, 353-355; *Looking for Spinoza*, 61-62, 73, 79-80, 99-101, 115-118, 137-150, 159, 160-175, 177-179, 276, 284.

CHAPTER FIVE

1. Here of course I differ with all who see the seven chakras as a one-way street from the gross to the supernatural, or supermind, what I call a Theosophical perspective. Examples would include Aldous Huxley's so-called "perennial philosophy" and the works of the always popular Huston Smith or Ken Wilbur. While there is much of value in their systems I believe they begin from an incorrect premise, that everything would cohere so neatly. *The Archetype of the Spirit* is as close as I come to making everything fit and here there is a great chaos of motifs and local traditions. The emerging fields of cognitive and neurological psychology show the integration of deep frames and "common sense" to be far more circumstantial and various, far more malleable than "a great chain of being" or a hierarchy of "holons." With exposures of "Descartes' Error" it is time to question "supermind" as well, to stay in touch with our embodied realities. See note 13.

2. Mircea Eliade, *Yoga: Immortality and Freedom* (New York: Pantheon Books, 1958), p. 117, 235.

    > . . . the cosmic skambha-pillar will be identified with the vertebral column; the "center of the world" will be found in a point (the "heart") or an axis (traversing the cakras) inside the body.

    > The point of departure for all these formulas was of course the transformation of the human body into a microcosmos, an archaic theory and practice, examples of which have been found almost all over the world. . . . The spinal column is identified with Mount Meru—that is, with the cosmic axis.

3. Joseph Campbell, *The Mythic Image* (New York: MJF Books, 1974), p. 288.

4. Ibid., pp. 282-283.

5. *Ephesians* 1: 20.

6. Solar divinities as we noted in Chapter Four are particularly the patrons of Kings and Emperors. As late as the fourth century while the Emperors had become Athanasian and Arian Christians, one, Julian the Apostate, reverted back to a pagan sun worship. See Bailey, pp. 308-313.

7. Edward L. B. Terrace, "A New Gallery of the Art of the Ancient East," Bulletin: Museum of Fine Arts, Boston Volume LVIII, 1960, No. 312, pp. 34-35.

8. Paul Bishop, *Jung's Answer to Job: A Commentary* (Hove: Brunner-Routledge, 2002), p. 173.

9. Arthur Avalon, *The Serpent Power* (New York: Dover Publications, 1974), p. 380. For discussion of the chakras, including the heart chakra, see Campbell, *The Mythic Image*, "The Lotus Ladder," pp. 330-391.

10. Numerous introductions to the Kabbalah and Sifirot exist, for example, Daniel C. Matt, *The Essential Kabbalah* (New York: Quality Paperback Book Club, 1995), and Z'ev ben Shimon Halevi, *Psychology and Kabbalah* (York Beach: Samuel Weiser, 1986).

11. Joseph Campbell, *The Inner Reaches of Outer Space* (New York: Harper & Row, 1986), pp. 93-100.

12. Isabel Briggs Myers *Introduction to Type, Sixth Edition* (Palo Alto: Consulting Psychologists Press, 1998), p. 42. See also Myers, *Gifts Differing*, pp. 175-176, 191.

13. For a discussion of this vertical bias towards sky see my *Four Spiritualities*, p. 164. The closing verse of the original version of Patanjali's *Yoga Sutras* (3: 55) reads:

    Absolute freedom occurs when the lucidity of material nature and spirit are in pure equilibrium.

    Barbara Stoler Miller, trans., *Yoga: Discipline of Freedom* (Berkeley: University of California Press, 1995), p. 73. Spiegelberg discusses the yoga principle of ascent and descent; see Frederic Spiegelberg, *Spiritual Practices of India* (New York: Citadel Press, 1962), pp. 63-65. This two direction process is implied in Joseph Campbell's discussion of the sun door and moon resurrection, "the yoga of world quitting," and "the yoga of world affirmation." Joseph Campbell, *Myths of Light* (Novato, CA: New World Library, 2003), p. 54. Campbell also discusses the Bardo traditions in *Transformations of Myth Through Time*, pp. 171-188, and in *The Mythic Image*, pp. 392-411. There are examples of the solar and lunar serpents where the solar serpent reverses direction with the head down and the tail up. Unfortunately these examples are rare. See p. 81.

14. *Luke* 18: 18-23.

15. See note 12 above, particularly Campbell, *Transformations of Myth Through Time*, pp. 171-188 and *The Mythic Image*, pp. 392-411.

CHAPTER SIX

1. John L. Giannini, *Compass of the Soul: Archetypal Guides to a Fuller Life* (Gainesville: Center for the Application of Psychological Type, 2004), pp. 243, 245.

2. Joseph Campbell, *Transformations of Myth Through Time*, 112-114.

3. Branko Bokun, *Man: The Fallen Ape* (New York: Doubleday & Company, 1977), pp. 110-112.

4. Thomas Cleary, trans., *The Secret of the Golden Flower* (New York: Harper San Francisco, 1991).

5. James Newman, *Figures to Accompany the Recorded Presentation of: Cognition and Consciousness: a Jungian Perspective on Mind and Brain* (Gainesville: Center for the Applications of Psychological Type, 1990), Figures 2, 3, 22, 23, 24, 25, 26.

6. Antonio Damasio, *Looking for Spinoza*, p. 35.

7. Carl Jung opens his autobiography with:

> My life is a story of the self-realization of the unconscious. Everything in the unconscious seeks outward manifestation, and the personality too desires to evolve out of its unconscious conditions and to experience itself as a whole.

Carl Jung, *Memories, Dreams, Reflections* (New York: Vintage Books, 1965), p. 3. As mentioned in chapter one, John Beebe attaches the anima/animus archetype to the fourth or inferior function. In Jung's words again:

> The essential thing is to differentiate oneself from these unconscious contents by personifying them, and at the same time to bring them into relationship with consciousness.

> The anima . . . communicates the images of the unconscious to the conscious mind. (p. 187)

It is no accident then that the inferior function is universally held to be the "doorway to the unconscious." Naomi Quenk emphasizes how important it is that the dominant function prevails and that the inferior function remains relatively undifferentiated. If not "we would lose the most precious connection with the unconscious through the inferior function. . ." Naomi Quenk, *Beside Ourselves*, p. 264. However, to the degree that a function is undifferentiated in consciousness, to a greater or lesser extent, there are up to eight doorways (Jung's eight function-attitudes). In early childhood before the dominant has become a strong center in consciousness, all eight it would seem may be in play at various times as "doorways." *In Memories, Dreams, Reflections*, the chapter "Confrontation with the Unconscious," Jung describes as a matter of scientific inquiry as well as personal crisis, that he "consciously submitted [him]self to the impulses of the unconscious." Looking back at age eighty he wrote:

> Today I am directly conscious of the anima's ideas because I have learned to accept the contents of the unconscious and to understand them. I know how I must behave toward the inner images. (p. 188)

8. *John* 17: 13-14.

9. *John* 15: 19.

10. *John* 17: 22-23.

11. The Sufi, Mansur Hallaj, for his affirmations, "I am the Truth" and "I am He," also suffered a martyr's death, in his situation by stoning. See Claud Field, *Mystics and Saints of Islam*, (London: Francis Griffiths, 1910), pp. 68-78.

12. *Bhagavad Gita* 2: 19-24.

13. José Ortega y Gasset, *Revolt of the Masses* (New York: W. W. Norton & Company, 1932), p. 76.

14. Reference here is to four of the five-fold sequence orders of consciousness as presented by Robert Kegan, a fertile theory when interfacing with psychological type. See Robert Kegan, *In Over Our Heads: The Mental Demands of Modern Life* (Cambridge: Harvard University Press, 1994), and with Lisa L. Lahey, *How the Way We Talk Can Change the Way We Work* (San Francisco: Jossey-Bass, 2001.)

15. In contrast, for example, Samuel Huntington, in his book, *The Clash of Civilizations*, theorizes there are nine world civilizations with fault lines keeping them apart: Western, Latin American, African, Islamic, Sinic, Hindu, Orthodox, Buddhist and Japanese. This theory is yet another "East is east and west is west and never the twain shall meet." Huntington counters the whole drama of human emergence on the planet and six thousand years of history recording the interdependence and mutuality of influence among the branches of human culture. Were his theory accurate the most basic assumptions of Jungian psychology and psychological type would be called into question, namely the collective unconscious and the universality of type as the differ-

entiation of human consciousness. It is true that the content and even orientations of enculturation in the various branches of culture is quite different. For example the differences between Western and Far Eastern thinking are illustrated by Richard Nisbett in his *The Geography of Thought* and by two outstanding translations of the Chinese classics, one by Ames and Rosemont, trans., *The Analects of Confucius* and the other by Ames and Hall, trans., *The Daode Jing*. Diversity among cultural centers is creative and gives us perspectives on our shared human nature. But we are one species and the long view makes us one culture with many family variations as well. For example, for a discussion of our inborn language faculty and what Noam Chomsky calls the human "Universal Grammar" see his *On Nature and Language* (Cambridge: Cambridge University Press, 2002). That Huntington's view supports contemporary political/cultural perspectives and prejudices is analogous to the role Thomas Malthus' analysis provided in a rationale for the exploits of the East India Company in the early nineteenth century (see R. Buckminster Fuller's *Operating Manual for Spaceship Earth*.) A far more imaginative view of cultural history can be found in William Irwin Thompson's *Imaginary Landscape: Making Worlds of Myth and Science* (New York: St. Martin's Press, 1989) in the chapter, "A Cultural History of Consciousness," pp. 125-169; and his *Transforming History: A Curriculum for Cultural Evolution* (Great Barrington: Lindisfarne Books, 2001).

16. Carl G. Jung, *The Archetypes and the Collective Unconscious* (Princeton: Princeton University Press, 1969), p. 167.

17. *Genesis* 1: 6-8.

18. A dramatic rendering of the life of King Saul is found in Julian Jaynes, *The Origin of Consciousness in the Breakdown of the Bicameral Mind* (Boston: Houghton Mifflin Company, 1976), pp. 306-308.

19. Composite. Near texts are in Christmas Humphreys, ed., *The Wisdom of Buddhism* (New York: Random House, 1961), p. 143 and John Daido Loori, *The Heart of Being* (Boston: Charles E. Tuttle Co., 1996), p. 132. The four Maha Bodhisattvas are met within the fifteenth chapter of *The Lotus Sutra*, translations of the Chinese text by Burton Watson; Leon Hurvitz; and Bunno, Kato, Tamura and Miyasaka. They are found in the fourteenth chapter in the Indian translation by H. Kern. Commentaries are helpful by Nikkyo Niwano, Thich Nhat Hanh, Shinjo Suguro and others. The Rissho Kosei-Kai movement in Japan has surrounding the central image of the Buddha, witnesses: the Tathagata Abundant Treasures and the four Maha Bodhisattvas, Jogyo, Muhengyo, Jogyo and Anryugyo. See *Rissho Kosei-kai* (Tokyo: Kosei Publishing Co., 1966), p. 26 and two plates showing the central image.

Olive tree near the Heraion of Argos, Greece.

"Cleopatra's Needle" so called, Olelisk from Heliopolis, Egypt, London, England.

Lakshmi, Chamun Deshwari Temple,
Belur, India.

BIBLIOGRAPHY

Note: Among the sources listed are selected scriptures. Here I have chosen one translation for each among my favorites but recommend multiple translations of any scripture.

Adams, James Luther, *Paul Tillich's Philosophy of Culture, Science & Religion*, 1965.

Ames, Roger T., & Rosemont, Henry, trans., *Analects of Confucius*, 1998.

Ames, Roger T., & Hall, David L., trans., *Dao De Jing*, 2003.

Arberry, A. J., trans., *The Koran*, 1955.

Armstrong, Karen, *The Great Transformation*, 2006.

Armstrong, Karen, *Muhammad: a Prophet for Our Time*, 2006.

Armstrong, Karen, *A History of God*, 1993.

Avalon, Arthur, *The Serpent Power*, 1974.

d'Alviella, Count Goblet, *The Migration of Symbols*, 1956.

Bailey, James, *The God-Kings & The Titans*, 1973.

Bataille, Georges, *The Cradle of Humanity: Prehistoric Art and Culture*, 2005.

Beebe, John, *A New Model of Psychological Types* (5 audio tapes), 1988.

Bokun, Branko, *Man: the Fallen Ape*, 1977.

Campbell, Joseph, *The Inner Reaches of Outer Space*, 1986.

Campbell, Joseph, *Myths of Light*, 2003.

Campbell, Joseph, *Pathways to Bliss*, 2004.

Campbell, Joseph, *Transformations of Myth Through Time*, 1990.

Camus, Albert, *The Rebel*, 1956.

Camus, Albert, *The Stranger*, 1959.

Chardin, Teilhard de, *The Phenomenon of Man*, 1959.

Cleary, Thomas, trans., *The Secret of the Golden Flower*, 1991.

Conze, Edward, *Buddhism: Its Essence and Development*, 1951.

Coomaraswamy, Ananda, *Buddha and The Gospel of Buddhism*, 1916.

Coward, Harold, *Yoga and Psychology*, 2002.

Creel, Herlee G., *Confucius and the Chinese Way*, 1949.

Crossan, John Dominic, *The Essential Jesus*, 1994.

Damasio, Antonio, *Descartes' Error*, 1994.

Damasio, Antonio, *The Feeling of What Happens*, 1999.

Damasio, Antonio, *Looking for Spinoza*, 2003.

Dewey, John, *A Common Faith*, 1934.

Drucker, Johanna, *The Alphabetic Labyrinth*, 1995.

Durkheim, Emile, *The Elementary Forms of the Religious Life*, 1915.

Eiseley, Loren, *The Firmament of Time*, 1960.

Eiseley, Loren, *The Immense Journey*, 1946.

Eiseley, Loren, *The Mind as Nature*, 1962.

Eliade, Mircea, *Patterns in Comparative Religion*, 1958.

Eliade, Mircea, *Yoga: Immortality and Freedom*, 1958.

Emerson, Ralph Waldo, *Essays*,

Enslin, Morton Scott, *From Jesus to Christianity*, 1964.

Enslin, Morton Scott, *The Prophet from Nazareth*, 1961.

Fingarette, Herbert, *Confucius: the Secular As Sacred*, 1972.

Foltz, Richard, *Religions of the Silk Road*, 1999.

Fowles, John, *The Aristos*, 1964.

Frankfort, Henri, et al, *Before Philosophy*, 1946.

Frankl, Viktor, *The Doctor and the Soul*, 1962.

Friedman, Edwin H., *A Failure of Nerve*, 1999.

Friedman, Edwin H., *Generation to Generation*, 1985.

Fromm, Erich, *You Shall Be as Gods*, 1966.

Fuller, R. Buckminster, *Critical Path*, 1981.

Fuller, R. Buckminster, *No More Secondhand God*, 1963.

Fuller, R. Buckminster, *Synergetics*, 1975 & 1979.

Giannini, John L., *Compass of the Soul*, 2004.

Goodall, Jane, *In the Shadow of Man*, 1988.

Gordon, Cyrus, *Before the Bible*, 1962.

Gordon, Cyrus, *Before Columbus*, 1971.

Guha, Ranajit, *History at the Limit of World-History*, 2002.

Guthrie, Stewart Elliott, *Faces in the Clouds*, 1993.

Haas, Leona, *Applying Type Dynamics Understanding Jung's Mental Processes*, 2003.

Haas, Leona & Hunziker, Mark, *Building Blocks of Personality Type*, 2006.

Hapgood, Charles H., *Maps of the Ancient Sea Kings*, 1966.

Harris, Anne Singer, *Living with Paradox: an Introduction to Jungian Psychology*, 1996.

Harris, Lee, *Civilization and Its Enemies: the Next Stage of History*, 2004.

Harris, Sam, *The End of Faith* 2005.

Hillman, James, *Insearch: Psychology and Religion*, 1967.

Hinton, David, trans., *Mencius*, 1998.

Hiriyanna, M., *Outlines of Indian Philosophy*, 1932.

Hirsh, Sandra and Kummerow, Jean, *Life Types*, 1989.

Humphreys, Christmas, ed., *The Wisdom of Buddhism*, 1960.

Huxley, Julian, *Religion Without Revelation*, 1957.

Jacobi, Jolande & Hull, R.F.C., eds., *C. G. Jung: Psychological Reflections*, 1970.

James, William, *Varieties of Religious Experience*, 1961.

Jaynes, Julian, *Origin of Consciousness in the Breakdown of the Bicameral Mind*, 1976.

Jung, Carl G., *Answer to Job*, 1958.

Jung, Carl G., *Mandala Symbolism*, 1959.

Jung, Carl G., *Memories, Dreams, Reflections*, 1961.

Jung, Carl G., *Psychological Types*, 1971.

Jung, Carl G., *Psychology and Religion*, 1938.

Kato, Brunno et al, trans., *The Three Fold Lotus Sutra*, 1975.

Kegan, Robert & Lahey, L., *How the Way We Talk Can Change the Way We Work*, 2001.

Kegan, Robert, *In Over Our Heads*, 1994.

Kriwaczek, Paul, *In Search of Zarathustra*, 2003.

Kroeger, Otto & Thuesen, Janet, *Type Talk*, 1988.

Lakoff, George & Johnson, Mark, *Metaphors We Live By*, 2003.

Lakoff, George & Johnson, Mark, *Philosophy in the Flesh*, 1999.

Lakoff, George, *Whose Freedom*, 2006.

Lal, P., trans., *The Dhammapada*, 1967.

Lee, Dorothy, *Freedom and Culture*, 1959.

Lewis, C. S., *The Abolition of Man*, 1947.

Lewis-Williams, David, *The Mind in the Cave*, 2002.

Mascaro, Juan, trans., *The Upanishads*, 1965.

Masuzawa, Tomoko, *The Invention of World Religions*, 2005.

McGinn, Colin, *The Mysterious Flame*, 1999.

McHale, John, *The Ecological Context*, 1970.

McHale, John, *The Future of the Future*, 1969.

McLuhan, Marshall, *Understanding Media*, 1964.

Merton, Thomas, trans., *The Way of Chuang-Tzu*, 1965.

Meyer, Marvin, trans., *The Secret Teachings of Jesus: Four Gnostic Gospels*, 1984.

Miller, Barbara S., trans., *The Bhagavad-Gita*, 1986.

Miller, Barbara S., trans., *Yoga: Discipline of Freedom (Patanjali)*, 1995.

Montagu, Ashley, *Education and Human Relations*, 1958.

Mumford, Lewis, *The Conduct of Life*, 1951.

Mumford, Lewis, *The Transformations of Man*, 1956.

Murray, Gilbert, *Five Stages of Greek Religion*, 1955.

Myers, Isabel Briggs, *Gifts Differing*, 1980.

Nanavutty, Piloo, trans., *The Gathas of Zarathushtra*, 1999.

Newman, James, *A Cognitive Perspective on Jungian Typology*, 1990.

Newman, James, *Cognition and Consciousness* (audio tapes), 1990.

Newman, James, *The Human Brain: A Frontier of Psychological Type* (audio tape).

Nikam, N.A.& McKoen, R., trans., *The Edicts of Asoka*, 1959.

O'Leary, DeLacy, *How Greek Science Passed to the Arabs*, 2001.

Patton, Kenneth L., *A Religion for One World*, 1964.

Patton, Kenneth L., *Chinese Humanism*, 1985.

Patton, Kenneth L., ed., *The Chinese Poets of Nature and Humanity*, 1984.

Patton, Kenneth L., ed., *Kaggen, the Mantis*, c.1986.

Patton, Kenneth L., ed., *The Way for This Journey*, 1976.

Polanyi, Michael, *The Tacit Dimension*, 1966.

Post, Laurens van der, *The Creative Pattern in Primitive Africa*, 1957.

Post, Laurens van der, *The Heart of the Hunter*, 1961.

Post, Laurens van der, *Jung & the Story of Our Times*, 1975.

Post, Laurens van der, *The Lost World of the Kalahari*, 1958.

Post, Laurens van der, *Patterns of Renewal*, 1962.

Progoff, Ira, *Jung's Psychology and Its Social Meaning*, 1953.

Quenk, Naomi L., *Beside Ourselves*, 1993.

Rahula, Walpola, *What the Buddha Taught*, 1974.

Randall, John Herman, *How Philosophy Uses Its Past*, 1963.

Revised Standard Version, *The Holy Bible*, 1946, 1952.

Richardson, Peter T., *Four Spiritualities*, 1996.

Richardson, Peter T., *Growing Your Spirituality*, 2001.

Riepe, Dale, *The Naturalistic Tradition in Indian Thought*, 1961.

Rosemont, Henry, Jr., *Rationality and Religious Experience*, 2001.

Rubenstein, Richard E., *Aristotle's Children*, 2003.

Rubenstein, Richard E., *When Jesus Became God*, 1999.

Russell, Bertrand, *A Free Man's Worship*, 1903.

Russell, Bertrand, *A History of Western Philosophy*, 1945.

Sanders, N. K., trans., *The Epic of Gilgamesh*, 1960.

Shlain, Leonard, *The Alphabet Versus the Goddess*, 1998.

Sinha, Phulgenda, *The Gita as It Was*, 1986.

Smith, Huston, *Essays on World Religion*, 1995.

Smith, Huston, *The World's Religions*, 1958.

Smith, Wilfred Cantwell, *Faith and Belief: the Difference Between Them*, 1979.

Smith, Wilfred Cantwell, *The Faith of Other Men*, 1963.

Smith, Wilfred Cantwell, *Modern Culture from a Comparative Perspective*, 1997.

Smith, Wilfred Cantwell, *Towards a World Theology*, 1981.

Smith, Wilfred Cantwell, *What Is Scripture?*, 1993.

Spoto, Angelo, *Jung's Typology in Perspective*, 1989.

Stein, Murray, *Jung's Map of the Soul*, 1998.

Stevens, Anthony, *On Jung*, 1999.

Sze, Mai-Mai, *The Tao of Painting*, 1956.

Tacey, David, *Jung and the New Age*, 2001.

Tagore, Rabindranath, *The Crescent Moon*, 1917.

Tagore, Rabindranath, *Gitanjali: Song Offerings*, 1916.

Tagore, Rabindranath, *The Religion of Man*, 1931.

Tagore, Rabindranath, *Sadhana: The Realization of Life*, 1913.

Thompson, Henry L., *Jung's Function-Attitudes Explained*, 1996.

Thompson, William Irwin, *At the Edge of History*, 1971.

Thompson, William Irwin, *Coming into Being*, 1996.

Thompson, William Irwin, *Passages About Earth*, 1974.

Thompson, William Irwin, *The Time Falling Bodies Take to Light*, 1981.

Thompson, William Irwin, *Transforming History*, 2001.

Watson, Burton, trans., *Hsun Tzu: Basic Writings*, 1963.

Watts, Alan W., *Nature, Man and Woman*, 1958.

Watts, Victor, trans., *Boethius: The Consolation of Philosophy*, 1969.

Weatherford, Jack, *Genghis Khan and the Making of the Modern World*, 2004.

Wilbur, Ken, *Integral Psychology*, 2000.

Wilbur, Ken, *Up from Eden*, 1981.

Wu-Chi, Liu, *A Short History of Confucian Philosophy*, 1955.

Wuthenau, Alexander von, *The Art of Terrracotta Pottery in Pre-Columbian Central and South America*, 1965.

Young, Dudley, *Origins of the Sacred*, 1991.

Yutang, Lin, *From Pagan to Christian*, 1959.

Yutang, Lin, *My Country and My People*, 1935.

Yutang, Lin, *The Importance of Living*, 1937.

Zimmer, Heinrich, *Myths and Symbols in Indian Art and Civilization*, 1946.

Zimmer, Heinrich, *Philosophies of India*, 1956.

Zweig, Stefan, *Erasmus and the Right to Heresy*, 1979.

CLOCKWISE FROM UPPER RIGHT *1) Redwoods, Yosemite National Park, CA; 2) tree at Bodh Gaya, India; 3) ancient cedars at Confucian Temple, Beijing, China; 4) bonsai tree, Huntington Museum, Passadena, CA*

Acknowledgements

In 1989 I qualified to administer the MBTI thanks to able teachers, Jean Kummerow and Judith Provost. Later Mary Thompson suggested to me the then "new" eight function- attitudes approach of John Beebe and I attended workshops led by Leona Haas. Gradually from type I absorbed the larger context of Jungian psychology. Jung's writing along with explorations by Joseph Campbell, Mircea Eliade and many others round out the preparations for this work.

I'd like to thank Dover Publications and others who have republished images in the public domain. In addition I have profound respect for museums which generously allow photography of our planetary inheritance: Egyptian Museum in Cairo, Egypt; National Museum in Valletta, Malta; Patna Museum in India; Museum of Natural History in Vienna, Austria; National Museum of Athens, Greece; British Museum, London, England; the Museum of Herakleion, Crete; and the Egyptian Museum, West Berlin, Germany.

It has once again been a pleasure to work with Amy Fischer of Camden in book design, with Dobromil Nosek for drawings of the figures as well as web design for **www.redbarnrockland.com**. Don Hester and Liz Hallows for reading the manuscript, and my wife Eleanor for her fine proof reading. Last but not least are many attending my workshops who have encouraged me to get this Archetype into book form. Thank you.

LEFT: *Palms, Naples, Florida*; RIGHT: *Pond, Andover, Massachusetts.*

INDEX

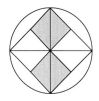

OTHER BOOKS BY THE AUTHOR

Four Spiritualities: A Psychology of Contemporary Spiritual Choice. Correlates four parallel patterns found within all branches of human religion with Jungian psychological type and the MBTI. Paperback, 245 pages, 10 illustrations, index, Davies-Black Publishing, 18.95.

Growing Your Spirituality: A workshop and seminar guide for applying Four Spiritualities to your life. Typescript, spiral bound, 166 pages, 8 illustrations. Red Barn Publishing, 12.00.

The Boston Religion: Unitarianism In Its Capital City. Describes Unitarian history, theology, sociology and interface with American culture, through the ministers and laity of Boston's 74 congregations. Hardbound, 264 pages, 139 illustrations, index. Red Barn Publishing, 29.95.

Exploring Unitarian Universalist Identity. The author's Minns Lectures for 2005, there are four chapters: (1) Finding Our Ground; (2) Congregational life: Standing Order, Free Association, Pluralism; (3) Transcendentalism and Its Transformations; and (4) From Unsectarian Sect to Multifaith Faith. Paperback, 121 pages, 16 illustrations, index. Red Barn Publishing, $14.95.

For more information visit **www.redbarnrockland.com**.

TO ORDER the above or additional copies of **Archetype of the Spirit** contact the author at Red Barn Publishing, 22 Mechanic Street, Rockland, ME 04841, 207-596-5502. Email to: PTEMR@aol.com.

www.redbarnrockland.com